FROM
LONELINESS
TO LOVE

FROM LONELINESS TO LOVE

A SPIRITUAL JOURNEY

PHIL NUERNBERGER, PH.D.

ELEMENT

Boston, Massachusetts • Shaftesbury, Dorset
Melbourne, Victoria

Text © Phil Nuernberger, Ph.D. 1999
© Element Books, Inc. 1999

Published in the USA in 1999 by
Element Books, Inc.
160 North Washington Street
Boston, MA 02114

Published in Great Britain in 1999 by
Element Books Limited
Shaftesbury, Dorset SP7 8BP

Published in Australia in 1999 by
Element Books Limited for
Penguin Australia Limited
487 Maroondah Highway, Ringwood, Victoria 3134

Library of Congress Cataloging-in-Publication Data available

ISBN 1-86204-356-6

Printed and bound in the United States by Courier

CONTENTS

DEDICATION

I DEDICATE THIS BOOK to my Gurudeva, His Holiness, Shri Swami Rama, the Tantric Tradition which he taught so masterfully, and to the lineage of great masters which he represented so compassionately during his life. I also want to dedicate this book to my parents, Irwin and Delores, and to my wife's parents, Bob and Betty Hoff. They have been, and are, shining examples of love for their children and grandchildren.

ACKNOWLEDGMENTS

NO ONE WRITES A BOOK without inspiration and support from many others. My wife, Deborah, my two daughters, Santosha and Raka, and my son, Samraj, have been an ever-present source of love and inspiration. Every day we share dreams and hopes and support each other's journey to freedom. With their courage, patience and love, they are truly a gift from the Divine. I have learned a great deal from my brother disciple, Charles Bates. He and I have shared the journey, and the master's teachings, from the very beginning. The same is true for my brother and sister disciples, Justin O'Brien and Theresa King. Their insights, laughter and support are irreplaceable. The love and sharing of close friends in the tradition, Barbara and Ricardo Melo and Mike and Nouhed Havrilla, provide an endless richness to life. My good friends, John and Dawn Harvey and Dick and Chris Roberts, continue to challenge me to grow. I particularly want to thank Noah Lukeman, my agent, whose generous time and effort played a key role in bringing this book to the public. And always, there is the Master, who has never left my heart. Whatever wisdom is in this book comes from him and the knowledge he has imparted. He continues to be the Light on my path.

INTRODUCTION

OF ALL THE DISEASES that plague mankind, loneliness is the greatest. It is a universal despair found in every culture and in every time. No one escapes the clutches of this dragon. We feel this loneliness in many ways: the emptiness of not having a partner or lover, the anxiety of being isolated from those we love, the depression when we face another holiday without family and friends, the ennui we experience in a crowd, even the silence in an elevator. Poetry and love songs captivate us because they somehow capture the universal despair of our loneliness.

The real tragedy of loneliness is that it is an illusion. "An illusion?" you say. "The feelings I have certainly are real enough. And people can suffer terribly from this disease, even commit suicide because of it." And you are right. Loneliness can have a very terrible impact, and the emotional disturbances—the sadness, the anxiety, the emptiness, the isolation—are very real. But these feelings are not loneliness, they are the anxieties of loneliness. And they arise out of the illusions we have about ourselves and about life.

Webster's Collegiate Dictionary denotes an illusion as something that deceives and misrepresents, that misleads us intellectually, "a perception of something objectively existing in such a way as to cause misinterpretation of its actual nature." And loneliness does all of this. Loneliness creates three illusions: isolation from others, from nature and from ourselves. Although they are very real problems, and create an endless variety of psychological and social problems, we are misled. We think that these problems of isolation are, in fact, loneliness, when in reality, they are only the symptoms of loneliness. We constantly try to resolve the symptoms, only to have loneliness rear its ugly head at another time, in another place. Therapists try to cure it, philosophers try to rationalize it and prostitutes make money off of it. We try to fend it off by having lovers and friends, getting married, having children, joining groups, getting religion, even going shopping. Yet, in the end, after all the lovers, after all the theories, after all the therapy, even with wonderful friends and loving families, the healthiest among us will feel the pangs of loneliness.

Loneliness is not an emotional problem, so all the therapy in the world will never cure it. Therapy may help in resolving some of the anxieties of loneliness, but it can never defeat the dragon itself. Even healthy people with successful relationships experience isolation and loneliness. Nor is loneliness a mental problem. Philosophy, higher education, science, none of these will protect us from the dragon. The philosopher's answer is to simply accept this condition and learn to live with it. They tell us that we must become stoic about our destiny, existentialist in our outlook. Bear up, they tell us, we all suffer, we are all essentially alone. Accept your fate and be strong. But loneliness doesn't happen because we are alone. In fact, we are often most lonely in a crowd of people. Being lonely and being alone, or in solitude, are two very different realities.

Loneliness stems from a universal human reality, the ego. The ego is a powerful function within every human mind that tells us we are unique individuals. The ego's task is to create a sense of separateness, an experience of unique individuality. I refer to this as the *ego-self* in the book. It is what we normally refer to as *me* or *I,* a pervasive sense of individuality locked within the boundaries of the body and mind. This is the grandest illusion of them all. We think we know who we are, and the truth is that we are not at all who we think we are. We mistakenly think we are the body and mind complex, when, in fact, these are only our tools.

We are not physical beings, we are spiritual beings. Loneliness is a spiritual problem, characterized by ignorance of the spiritual Self within each and every one of us. When all we know is the material ego-self, when all we experience is physical sensations and mental thoughts and emotions, then we do not realize that our rightful heritage is the eternal core of our being, the spiritual Self. We can call it soul, Consciousness, a spark of the Divine Light; the name is irrelevant, as it is only a name. But freedom lies in the experience of this spiritual Self. To free ourselves from this universal misery called loneliness, we must make a spiritual journey; we must experience, for ourselves, our spiritual Self.

We have three powerful tools for spiritual awakening. Prayer, the path of the heart, loosens the grip of the ego by creating a profound sense of humility and acknowledgment. Through prayer we prepare the mind for enlightenment, the mystical experience of pure love. Along with prayer, we access our inner strength through meditation, the path of the mind. By refining the power of concentration through meditation, we pass through the veil of the mind and consciously experience the mystical Self. A new identity emerges from this powerful, mystical experience of Divine Union, and we realize the underlying unity of all life. The third tool is contemplation, the path of the intellect. By refining the power of our pure intellect, we realize that life itself is nothing less than the dance of the Divine.

This mystical experience is called love. This is not the love that we normally seek, which is part of the illusion. It is a common myth that loneliness arises out of a need to be loved, to share life with another. While we must acknowledge the human need for companionship and to be loved, being loved will never solve the problem of loneliness. This need creates even greater emotional dependency, building and reinforcing weakness in the ego-self. This, in turn, only leads to greater isolation and loneliness.

We do need to be loved, most particularly in childhood. Love is necessary in order to create a healthy ego, one that is capable of returning love and building satisfying relationships. But satisfying the need for love does not protect us from being lonely. In an odd way, it makes loneliness even stronger.

You see, it isn't getting love that counts, but the act of loving itself. This is not what the therapists refer to as self-love, the limited, ego-centered focus of attention on the personal self. It is, rather, the expression and the power of our spiritual core, the mystical Self. In this loving, there is no sense of personal identity, no small self to take credit. Only through the mystical experience of being pure love will loneliness and the anxiety and fears created by the ego's sense of separateness be completely resolved. It is called "mystical" because it is beyond the mind and body, beyond the explanation of logic and the limited scope of material science. It is understood *only* by having the experience itself.

The mystical experience is actually the most practical way of life. It provides us with the knowledge to create a successful life. In the final chapter, selflessness, the character of pure love, is translated into practical guidelines for day-to-day living. We cannot avoid the trials and challenges of life, but through spiritual knowledge we can transform our lives into ones of love, joy and tranquillity.

Through the mystical experience, we discover that we are already the love we seek. It is this mystical experience alone—not logic and degrees, not philosophy or psychology, not religious belief—that brings freedom from the tyranny of our ego-imposed loneliness. Through prayer, meditation and contemplation, we discover the selfless love of our mystical Self. It is then, and only then, that we realize that life itself is the expression of this spiritual force, and life becomes the spiritual path. Free of the limitations of the small ego-centered self, we embark joyfully upon a spiritual journey armed with the courage, strength and wisdom of pure love.

What is presented in this book is not theory, but a record of my own personal journey. The quotes at the beginning of each chapter were told to me by my spiritual master. His example, teaching and love were the strength of my journey. My hope is that the words in this book will, in some small way, pass on his wisdom, knowledge and love to you. The book is not intended as a therapy, nor is it a philosophical position. It is a practical approach to spiritual Self-realization. It is a journey which all may take. There are no obstacles but ourselves. We create the mountains and we climb them. It is a journey, taken step by step through self-mastery, to Self-realization. Take the journey. Discover the joy. Become the Love.

*The practice of love is the
natural awareness of God.*
—Swami Rama

CHAPTER I

ALONE IN A CROWD

Loneliness is the greatest disease of mankind.

"LONELINESS is the greatest disease of mankind." I listened to my spiritual master say these words many times before I realized the truth of what he was saying. For a long time, I thought the statement was a bit of an exaggeration. Sure, I reasoned, we all have times when we feel isolated and alone, and some people seem to be very lonely—those who lack family ties; people who are shy and have difficulty meeting others and building friendships; lovers who are separated; people alone during the holidays. But for the most part, loneliness seemed to be just another emotional disturbance, and not the most serious one at that.

Only after I studied with my spiritual master for a couple of years did I finally recognize the truth of his statement. The first time I was forced to confront my own loneliness face-to-face was in the early evening of a beautiful spring day. I was with my master, preparing to return to my apartment in another city several hundred miles away. The time I spent with him, filled with the power of his love and knowledge, was precious to me. I had spent several days with him, listening, watching and learning. But it was time for me to return to my work and I was savoring every minute I could be with him until it was time to leave.

As usual, he was using the time wisely, teaching me, in so many ways, to become more aware of the realities within myself. We were talking about the programs we were preparing for the Institute, the organization he had established to bring yoga as a science to the West.

He suddenly stopped talking and was quiet for a moment. He then looked at me with the greatest love and tenderness and said, "You are very lonely, aren't you?" I was stunned. These words, spoken with the greatest compassion, ripped into my heart. I struggled to keep from crying as this simple truth forced me to come face-to-face with my own loneliness.

I could no longer hide from the powerful, frightening dragon of loneliness. At that moment, it came roaring, breathing flame and smoke into my awareness. It was one of the most peculiarly painful moments in my life. I have experienced the deaths of family and friends, and my sadness at their passing was consuming and powerful. Like everyone, I have suffered losses and disappointments, felt the pain of regret and tasted defeat. I have had to confront and battle fear and self-hatred that hid in the corners of my mind. But of all these things, nothing was sharper, more pervasive and more painful than this sudden revelation of loneliness.

The last few moments I had with him are still a blur in my mind. But I clearly remember the plane ride home. I thought to myself that I never wanted to see my master again! I didn't want any more revelations involving this kind of pain. Thankfully, those thoughts lasted only as long as the plane ride itself. But they revealed just how difficult, how painful and how powerful this loneliness was. Of the three great dragons of the mind—fear, self-hatred and loneliness—loneliness is the most powerful, the most pervasive, the most subtle and the most painful.

Like most people, I thought that I was lonely because I didn't have a partner, someone to love me and share my life with. I thought love was all about finding the "right" person, and making that person yours —a matter of mutual ownership. As a consequence, I was possessive and easily became jealous. I was always involved in at least one intense relationship, but I found a reason to resist the commitment necessary to build a lasting relationship. Marriage seemed like an unreasonable burden of responsibility, so I never allowed things to become too serious. Consequently, I was never able to really give of myself in these relationships. As I look back, I was clearly a very lonely person.

About a year after the confrontation with my loneliness, my spiritual master confronted me with another issue I was avoiding. He told me that I should be married. I really didn't want to hear that. What I really wanted, I told him, was to become enlightened (whatever that meant!). He insisted that I should be married as well as enlightened, and that he would "open my third eye" and that I would have a vision of the woman I would marry sometime in the future. Naturally, I was quite intrigued with this possibility. I love to have new experiences, particularly unusual ones. And I must admit, I was also intrigued by the idea of having a vision of the person I was to marry.

A few months later, I had a very strange vision while meditating. A woman I knew, who was also studying in my tradition, appeared and told me that my spiritual master had sent her to show me the woman I was to marry. In the vision, she took me into a high-school classroom where I sat in the last seat in a row. In came a beautiful blond teacher, her hair done up in a ponytail. She gave me a wonderful smile, and the vision abruptly ended. Needless to say, I was more than a little interested.

A year and a half passed, and no one even faintly resembling the beautiful woman in my vision entered my life. I was busy studying and teaching with my master, as well as running a biofeedback program as part of a chronic pain study in a neurology clinic. One of my patients asked me if his neighbor's daughter could talk to me about the program. She had just graduated from college, was interested in biofeedback, and wanted to see how it worked in a clinical setting. I told him that she should make an appointment with my secretary. Since I ran one of the first clinical biofeedback programs in the country, I was used to having other professionals and interested people pop in to see how we used biofeedback to treat chronic pain problems.

Then she arrived for her appointment—a beautiful, blond woman, her hair arranged in a ponytail. She looked at me and smiled. It was the face I had seen in my vision. She said she was a high-school teacher and was interested in biofeedback. After talking for two hours, it was clear that there was a great deal more between us than a fascination with biofeedback. We started dating that weekend. Three months later, she went to Chicago with me to meet my spiritual master. We walked into his small house and sat on the floor in front of him. He looked at me, then looked at her, and then looked back at me. Without so much as hello, he said directly to me, "If you don't marry her, I will never advise you about women again!"

Fortunately, the woman who would become my wife had already decided that she wanted to marry me. I must admit that I was in a bit of shock, but I knew in my heart that my master had given the right advice. Six months later we were married, and by the time we celebrated our first anniversary, we had the first of three beautiful, independent and talented children. I was certain that I would never be lonely again.

But all the love I received from family and friends didn't end the feelings of loneliness. As most of us discover, having lovers, friends and family doesn't solve the problem. It is a great illusion to believe that all we need to make all our loneliness disappear is to find someone who will love us. When we find someone to love and to love us, nothing really changes. We will be distracted for a while, but eventually the same old pangs of loneliness return.

After becoming aware of the profound sense of loneliness within me, I continued to study and practice the disciplines of tantra yoga under the personal guidance of my master. Through my practices, I began to realize that fears, anxieties and self-hatred are not a necessary part of life, but simply powerful habits that take root in the mind. They are not inherent or innate truths of the human personality. In other words, we are not born with fear and self-hatred. We develop these emotional disturbances as we grow up. They are not permanent parts of the human personality. More important, I discovered that the anxiety and emptiness we experience when we feel unloved and alone are certainly painful and difficult emotions, but they are only the symptoms of loneliness, not the problem itself. Loneliness, at its root, is not an emotional problem at all. Loneliness is caused by a source more powerful and pervasive than the emotions. It lies within the ego function of the mind. The ego is a necessary part of the human personality, but it remains a source of difficulty and confusion until it is understood fully.

Becoming aware of this loneliness was only the first step. It took me a long time to free myself from its grip. As I became more skilled in the meditative practices of the tantric tradition, I realized that loneliness is only the surface of a profound human condition of ignorance. As my master initiated me into the deeper spiritual mysteries of our tradition, I became aware of the eternal nature of the spiritual Self, the unseen, unrecognized eternal power that lies within each and every one of us. But even as I gained greater freedom from fear and self-hatred, loneliness remained a problem. Even when surrounded by love, I sometimes felt alone, isolated and misunderstood. The face of the dragon remained hidden in the subtle, unexplored smoke and shadows of my mind.

I struggled with this dragon until my last trip, with my master, to Nepal. There, on the side of a mountain, he initiated me into the highest paths of our tradition, permanently opening the inner pathways to the spiritual core. In this initiation, I realized the truth of the biblical phrase "I and my Father are One." The dragon, with all its power and fury, disappeared. Only then, in the light of the spiritual Self, could I see that loneliness is nothing more than an illusion, a false reality that thrives in the darkness of spiritual ignorance.

Without the spiritual awareness gained through the disciplines and wisdom of tantra yoga, I would have never become free from loneliness. Tantra yoga is an exploration and discipline of the mind. Its goal is Self-realization through self-mastery, the cumulation of self-knowledge, self-discipline and skill. Much of what is said and written about tantra in the West is sheer nonsense. Tantra demands discipline, experimentation and verification. Belief is irrelevant, and direct experience is considered to be the only basis of true knowledge. The purpose of tantra is to gain complete awareness and knowledge of the Divinity as it expresses Itself in daily life. The great insights of tantric mystics are based on a penetrating understanding of body, mind and spirit. Tantric practices are found in all spiritual traditions, including Christianity and Judaism. You don't have to become a tantric mystic to become free of loneliness. Nor must you change your religious persuasion. It is not a matter of belief, but of experience, knowledge and discipline. Travelers of all traditions are welcome on this journey.

HOW LONELINESS AFFECTS US

No one, regardless of culture, race or belief, is exempt from the condition of loneliness. Don't underestimate its power. It generates self-hatred, insensitivity to ourselves and indifference to others, leading to disease and even suicide. Yes, loneliness even affects physical health. In his book, *The Broken Heart*, Dr. James Lynch documents how loneliness can lead to serious heart disease and other illnesses. Other researchers report that people who lack social support have a higher death rate from all diseases. Dr. Dean Ornish, a cardiologist, has proven that experiencing social support is just as important as diet and exercise in curing heart disease.

In fact, loneliness can be lethal. We can become so isolated that we see no further purpose in living. Loneliness and isolation play a major role in the high incidence of teenage suicide. The pressures on teenagers—drugs, materialism, performance and social demands—seem to increase with every generation, and few are given the emotional and spiritual skills they need to cope with these challenges. Many of these teenagers come from middle-class families with wonderful material and educational opportunities. This doesn't change the desperate sense of isolation they feel.

Loneliness breeds fears, anger and greed. Material success doesn't protect us from loneliness. In fact, it often makes it worse. When you have everything you could need or want and still feel isolated and alone, the effects can be devastating. Loneliness often leads to apathy toward the environment. When we don't feel connected to nature as part of the amazing web of life, we become careless and callous toward nature. Our greed to accumulate more and more possessions is nothing more than a feeble attempt to compensate for what we have lost in our isolation from our inner selves, other people and nature. The frenzied quest to gain material wealth is part of the illusion. When we walk along the beach, in the forest or in the mountains, we seldom feel any need to buy more and more things. We experience the calming, healing qualities of nature. But when we return to our hectic lives, we forget nature in our quest to acquire bigger cars, more clothes, fancier homes. The struggle for material gain obscures the natural wealth and balance that is already there for us.

FROM ILLUSION TO UNDERSTANDING

Loneliness is subtle. Often we only recognize it through its most typical symptoms of anxieties and depression. But fortunately, in the end, loneliness can be understood and mastered. Discovering and accessing the spiritual Self brings illusion to an end, along with the pain, misery and disease that it causes. As we become conscious of our spiritual core, we free ourselves from loneliness and its painful symptoms.

No one else can do this for us. It is an individual responsibility and journey that requires knowledge, effort and skill. But each of us can travel the path to freedom. The first step is to clearly understand the three specific illusions that cloud our thinking about loneliness.

THE FIRST ILLUSION: WE NEED THAT SPECIAL SOMEONE TO BE HAPPY

The first illusion is the most familiar condition. It is the loneliness we feel when we don't have the comfort, contact and love provided by another human being. Isolation from others makes us desire a partner —someone to love us, make us feel important and encourage us. When we don't have that "special someone," we feel lonely, unloved, unwanted and unneeded. At certain times, these feelings of isolation can become so intense that suicide may seem preferable to facing the loneliness day after day. This is particularly true during the holiday season when everyone seems to be happy except us.

Sometimes people have good reasons for feeling lonely. Lack of success in building friendships, a failing marriage, isolation from family, or deaths among family and friends as one grows older can leave a person in a social vacuum. These are all genuine problems that can be resolved in a number of ways—psychotherapy and counseling, broadening social circles and developing new friendships, even helping others in a volunteer capacity. If we don't see life problems as opportunities for growth and positive change, they become a source of despair and helplessness, and loneliness gains the upper hand.

We also fantasize about the perfect romance. It's practically an addiction in our society. We express our loneliness and longing for idealized fulfillment in love songs in various styles, from country music to opera. The desire to stave off loneliness through finding the perfect mate has fueled many profit-making enterprises: TV soap operas, romance novels, dating services, self-help seminars, singles bars and other purveyors of fantasy. Too often we are willing dupes to these chimeras. We distract ourselves with new friends and lovers, join organizations and stay as busy as possible to avoid painful introspection and alleviate the anxieties of our loneliness and isolation.

We are vulnerable to these simplistic solutions because loneliness is so difficult to bear. It produces powerful emotions that make us want to escape and dull the pain. We become so entangled in emotional reactions that we completely overlook the deep cause of the anxiety. We focus on our feelings, persuaded that they are the problem. Unfortunately, these emotions are only the symptoms, and as long as we focus on them, we will never understand the underlying problem. It's like having a headache and taking an aspirin to make it go away; if you don't solve the chronic tension that causes the headache, after a while the headache returns and you will have to take another aspirin.

When we find someone to cling to, the loneliness seems to go away. Getting married and having a family work at least for awhile in convincing us that we are no longer alone, that we are important to someone, that we *belong!* Life takes on new meaning; we find joy in every little thing, and it seems that these feelings will last forever.

One of the dangers of this condition is dependency. We become convinced that we must have that "special person" in order to feel complete, happy and secure. But soon it's not enough to have found a loving partner. The special person must behave in certain ways in order to make us happy. We impose unrealistic expectations on the "loved one" who, in turn, gives us the same treatment. As expectations escalate, so does unhappiness.

The more we depend on others, the more we try to protect our investments. Instead of loving people, we begin to own them. People lose their status as individuals and become objects that we use to satisfy our needs. In some instances, this behavior becomes pathological, resulting in all-too-familiar situations like that of the controlling husband who dominates his wife's every move and thought. Abusive relationships and jealousies are only the more dramatic problems created by emotional dependency. They produce abuse and loss of trust. Relationships become contractual, quid pro quo arrangements, producing prenuptial agreements and abundant financial returns for lawyers.

Loneliness is not caused by the lack of someone to love us. We find the truth of this in our own experience. No matter how many lovers we have, sooner or later we find ourselves with the same old feelings. After the initial glow starts to wane, after the newness wears off and the giddiness diminishes, after the celebration has settled into routine day-to-day activities, the dragon begins to stir—subtle feelings of isolation and loneliness, of not being understood, of being taken for granted and feeling that you can't communicate honestly about your doubts and uncertainties. "The perfect mate" seldom lives up to expectations, and we find that even marriage is no protection from loneliness.

Some people conclude that loneliness and isolation are just part of life, that nothing can be done about them. They become stoical philosophers and learn to live with the difficulties. Others find a therapist to help them discover the "inner child," suggest more effective ways to build friendships or help locate support groups. Therapy is useful for learning more effective social skills, overcoming personal habits that interfere with healthy relationships and resolving anxieties to become happier, more successful human beings. It can help us with emotional problems. But emotions are not the cause of loneliness.

The therapeutic approach to curing loneliness doesn't really work, just as taking an aspirin never really cures the headache. It only treats the symptom. We can find someone to love us, make new friends, fill our minds with positive imagery, abolish our self-hatred and fears, learn coping skills and release our inner child. But in the end, our loneliness returns. We may end up spending time and money on every new-age fad that comes along, from wearing the right crystal to increasing our sexual skills, in a misdirected attempt to reach a constant emotional (and even physical) cosmic orgasm. We end up exhausted, cynical, despairing and with a thinner wallet. We have done nothing to change the fundamental loneliness that caused the symptoms.

Loneliness is not an emotion, even though we feel emotional when we are lonely. As long as we think of loneliness as an emotional problem, it's cure seems to lie in finding others to love and care for us, in making friends or in joining some group. But we are engaging an illusion. The actual cause of our negative feelings is the sense of separateness created by the ego. This is the true face of the dragon, hidden in the smoke and mirrors of the mind and hard to discern. Consequently, it is difficult to free ourselves from its clutches.

THE SECOND ILLUSION: IDENTIFYING WITH THE HABITS OF THE MIND

The second illusion involves the loneliness we feel because we are unaware of our inner strengths. It is characterized by the beliefs, emotional patterns and attitudes that constitute our self-concept. For most, this self-concept has little to do with their actual personal qualities. They are only habits, patterns of "mind-stuff" that are generally learned in childhood and, for the most part, remain unchallenged throughout our adult life. Deep introspection is not part of Western culture, and most people simply do not have the necessary self-awareness skills to look more deeply into themselves. Consequently, they identify with superficial patterns in the mind and rarely discover their more powerful and beautiful qualities.

If our self-concepts are healthy, we go through life successfully. We trust our instincts, express our feelings and share openly with others. But when these patterns are destructive—characterized by self-doubt, self-hatred, fears and anxieties—they create misery, sabotage success and interfere with relationships. Critical of ourselves, we fear criticism from others, and as we protect ourselves from possible hurts, we become even more isolated from others. Life becomes increasingly difficult as we try to cope with the challenges, while using, perhaps, less than five percent of our true capacity.

Many times we compensate by trying to live in the images of who we should be. This only increases our isolation, leading to even more fear and loneliness. We become constantly insecure, distrusting our instincts and intuitions, and we lack inner strength, self-respect and self-esteem. Uncomfortable with ourselves, we are uncomfortable with others. We become fearful and anxious that somehow we just aren't good enough. But in truth, we worry that we won't be accepted for who we are because we don't accept who we are. We feel this in the awkwardness of silence when a conversation takes a long pause, in the silence on an elevator as it moves between floors or in the silent anxiety when the subway stops between stations.

When we are unaware of our own strengths, we become more and more dependent on the approval of others. We join and cling to groups, expecting them to provide a substitute identity. We begin to see those who differ from us as dangerous and threatening. As fear makes us increasingly more rigid, we become even more isolated and fearful, and even more dependent on approval from the group. These fears and group identities can become so strong that they become the basis for violence and war.

Still others seek approval by always trying to be "nice." They "sacrifice for others," they struggle to be rich, powerful and important, to have their "fifteen minutes of fame," to *be someone*—all in a vain attempt to compensate for inner insecurity and isolation. And yet, for all their importance, still they wake in the quiet of the night feeling alone and isolated. This agony is reflected in what Frank Sinatra once reportedly said: "I'm for anything that gets you through the night—pills, women or booze."

Here again, many of us turn to therapy for help. Therapy can help us gain greater insight into ourselves and greater control over our emotions, allowing us to grow in self-respect and self-worth and to diminish the pain caused by self-isolation. But therapy is limited to the material self, the mind/body complex that constitutes the personality. We can build new images to live in, ones that are more effective socially and personally. But they are still images, beliefs and patterns in a mind that is still controlled and dominated by the ego-self. Because therapy is not a spiritual practice, it will not lead to the spiritual knowledge necessary to defeat the dragon. Therapy can enhance emotional maturity, but the deep cause of loneliness remains untouched.

We read self-help books that tell us to express our "inner child," indulge our whims and desires, that we have a right to be self-centered and seek pleasure. Therapists tell us that we must learn to love ourselves and build self-esteem. After all, it is true that without self-respect, we cannot respect others. And unless we love ourselves, we cannot love others. All of this sounds like very good advice.

But this advice overlooks a very subtle trap. The more we focus on ourselves, the more self-centered we become. And self-centeredness fuels loneliness. We should indeed love and respect ourselves, but we can't do that by being self-centered. Nor is self-esteem created through self-indulgence and pleasure-seeking. Certainly we need to take care of ourselves, but we must also understand the difference between self-care and self-indulgence. Self-esteem isn't created by self-praise, but through skillful self-expression. It is futile to try to build self-esteem without the discipline and self-knowledge necessary to support it. It is here that the great spiritual traditions, with their emphasis on self-discipline and self-knowledge, have far more to offer than any therapeutic approach.

We are not who we *think* we are. Our thoughts and beliefs have no reality outside of the mind. We may believe ourselves to be powerless, unattractive, incapable, unlovable, worthless. And if we accept this illusion as "the truth," it holds power over us. These conditioned patterns of the mind become our reality. If I believe that I am weak, ineffectual and powerless, I will behave in a weak, ineffectual and powerless way. But they are *only* beliefs, and mind-garbage beliefs to boot. They are not the reality. To put an end to the illusion, we must reach beyond the mind-stuff, and discover the truth about who we really are.

THE THIRD ILLUSION: WE ARE SEPARATE FROM NATURE

One more illusion prevents us from understanding loneliness: the separation we create between us and nature. The ego tells us that we are to conquer nature, that we are its keeper. But in fact we are part of nature itself. Isolation from nature allows us to destroy our environment, create water and air pollution and rape and pillage our natural resources to achieve short-term gain. We lose touch with the rhythms of life and think and behave mechanistically. In our egocentric view, we see ourselves superior to the very nature that protects and nourishes us. We don't realize that when we abuse nature, we abuse ourselves. If we don't overcome this illusion, we may find that we have spoiled our own nest to such a degree that we can no longer live in it.

We experience the loneliness caused by isolation from nature as feelings of disharmony and restlessness. To compensate, we shop! We buy material things to achieve some sense of satisfaction, harmony and balance. The more rich and powerful we become, the greater and more expensive our toys. But the more things we acquire, the more isolated we become from the rhythms of nature, and the more restless we feel. We become fearful of the dark, uncomfortable in natural surroundings and ignorant of our environment.

I remember an incident involving two colleagues from New York City who worked with me on developing an audiocassette tape. The private sound studio we were using was located in isolated farm country. We spent the day working on the tape. By the time we were finished, it was late in the evening. We opened the door and stepped out on the porch into a beautiful, clear night with no moonlight at all. It was beautifully, wonderfully dark. The two New Yorkers huddled together, holding on to each other as they made their way to their car. I'm not sure what they thought was going to come out of the dark at them, but they could hardly wait to get back to city lights.

We all have experienced the power of nature to heal, to calm, to invite us into harmony and balance. When we return to nature—to walk in the forest, lie on the beach, hike in the mountains—we feel balanced and rested. The harmony of nature draws out the harmony within ourselves. We feel refreshed, ready to take on the next task. In these moments we no longer feel isolated from ourselves or others.

Often those whose work is closely tied to the seasons of nature reflect its calmness and wisdom. I think of Ben Garing, a dairy farmer in northeastern Pennsylvania. Thoughtful and slow-speaking, Ben is a successful dairy farmer. When I first moved to the area, I contacted Ben to buy some firewood from him. As I got to know him, I began to understand why he is called Gentle Ben by his community. With natural wisdom and balance, Ben knows just how to make the person around him feel comfortable and appreciated. Once, we were unloading a truckful of firewood just after Ben had slaughtered a cow, and he asked if I would like to buy some of the fresh beef.

"Well, Ben, I don't think so," I replied. "I don't eat meat of any kind and haven't for about twenty years."

"You don't eat any beef or pork?" Ben asked incredulously. "No chicken or fish?"

"Nope, not a bite for a long time," I replied.

"Well," he said, "you must be one of them vegetarians. Is that right?"

"That's right, Ben. I am a vegetarian," I replied as we continued to throw wood off the truck.

Ben was silent for a few moments. Then he turned to me and said, "Well, you don't seem too strange to me."

Over the years, I took my children to Ben's farm to watch the cows and feed the chickens. He shared with me his love of Gene Autry's music, and he still continues to provide me with firewood and manure for my gardens. With every load, Ben brings me something extra—some grapes from his vineyard, a dozen eggs, a few kind words.

Now retired and in his early seventies, Ben carries a great sadness. His son will not be continuing the dairy farm that has been in the family for generations. Ben realizes that, in all likelihood, he is the last dairyman of the family farm. Ben carries his sadness with a dignity that reflects the strength of his nature. A lifetime of living in harmony with the seasons and rhythms of nature has given him an understanding and acceptance of change, time and timelessness that even this disappointment cannot diminish. Gentle Ben is one of the wealthiest men I have ever known—not in money, fortune or fame, but in character, strength and endurance. His priorities are in order. Ben knows that if you "take care of the roof, you'll always have a good barn," an adage that is exemplified by the still-pristine, well-maintained barn built by his great-grandfather over 120 years ago.

Time in nature can raise our awareness of the reality deep within ourselves. We sense something far greater than the petty needs and fears harbored by ego, something that resonates with the harmony and balance of nature. Nature helps us approach the heart of the spiritual

Self, the inner strength that frees us from loneliness and isolation.

We can't solve the problem of loneliness as long as we confuse illusions with reality. As long as we focus on the emotional and physical symptoms of loneliness instead of understanding its true source, we will continue to suffer. Loneliness has nothing to do with others, although we often are most lonely in a crowd of people. Instead, the source of our loneliness is the crowd of illusions that exist in our own mind. When we find our way through the smoke and mirrors of the mind and discover the light of the spiritual Self, the darkness clears away. The anxieties we thought so powerful and compelling disappear in the light of our experience and knowledge. Let us now explore how the mind works, and we will discover how loneliness is created.

CHAPTER 2

THE FACE OF THE BEAST

*When you deny your nature, the outcome is
profound loneliness.*

WHEN WE DISPEL the illusions that masquerade as explanations
for loneliness, we come face-to-face with the real heart of the problem: the conscious realization of our unique individuality and
separateness. This experience can be so overwhelming that we often
hide from it, preferring the more familiar anxiety created by the illusions. It usually takes a crisis to make us realize that no one will, or
even can, experience the pain and suffering we feel. We cannot take
refuge in another person, in wealth or possessions, or in an enhanced
self-image. We experience and understand clearly our unique individuality and separateness. We recognize that we are, in a sense, truly
alone. This fundamental and inescapable fact of life is experienced by
each and every human mind regardless of culture, race, sex or belief.
From this source arises all the negative emotions and thoughts we normally think of as loneliness.

Loneliness is universal because every human being has a mind and
experiences himself or herself as being a unique individual. Loneliness
is the inevitable outcome of having an individual identity, that sense
of "I-ness" that tells me that I am myself, different and unique from
everyone else. The more emphasis and value we place on individual
achievement, the greater the intensity of loneliness and isolation we
experience. But even those in Eastern cultures, which traditionally
place an emphasis on community rather than individuality, suffer from
loneliness.

If we are strong and healthy emotionally, we accept this as a fundamental fact of life and create loving relationships and families, participate in community efforts and become loving members of our communities. This is all well and good, but it does not solve the problem of loneliness. Lurking below the surface, the dragon is still alive and well. We must explore the human psyche to unlock the true nature of the problem.

THE FUNCTIONS OF THE MIND

The first step out of illusion is to grasp what is really happening when we feel isolated from our own self. The key to understanding and overcoming loneliness is to first become familiar with the workings of the human mind, especially the powerful function called ego. We don't need fancy psychological theories to explain the mind. A simple framework of its basic functions will provide the insight we need to solve the problems of anxiety and loneliness. The more we know about how the mind works, the more skilled we will become at resolving many problems. After all, the mind is the finest instrument that we have. The term "instrument" is appropriate because we use the mind to create knowledge, to be successful in life. Everything we think, everything we know, comes from using it. The mind is an inner instrument, whereas the body is the outer instrument.

To perform its many tasks—processing sensory information, creating emotional reactions, analyzing and building knowledge, remembering, stimulating action—the mind utilizes four powerful functions: sensory, memory, discrimination and ego functions. They direct the different activities of the mind so we can form knowledge, understand the world around us and do what we choose to do.

The functions of the mind do not act separately. The mind operates as a single, whole entity. In every activity, every function contributes its influence. For example, say you are walking across a field, in the distance, you see a large animal with horns coming in your direction (sensory function). You immediately recognize this creature as a bull (memory function). You also realize that the bull is running toward you (discriminating function). And you think, "Hey, this bull is attacking me!" (ego function). Of course, your innate drive for self-preservation is going to stimulate a great deal of energy (motivation), and without lengthy consideration, you begin to run as fast as you can for the fence.

These four functions play different roles in determining whether or not we feel the anxieties caused by loneliness. As we explore these functions, we will discover how we create emotional problems and how they can be easily solved. More important, we will discover the actual cause of loneliness, and realize that it too is just another illusion.

SENSORY AND MEMORY FUNCTIONS: THE POWER TO FEEL GOOD OR BAD

The sensory and memory functions play an important role in whether or not we suffer from the anxieties of loneliness. The sensory function is a very busy and noisy function, involving four powerful activities—perception, language, emotions and habit. It is responsible for collecting, organizing and interpreting sensory data and creating meaning out of it. The memory function plays a crucial role in helping the sensory mind create our personal sense of reality. Only a small part of this function represents what we normally think of as memory—the ability to recall information. The memory function primarily serves as the storehouse of all our experiences. Every experience that we pay attention to, good or bad, is stored in the mind. These past experiences provide the backdrop against which we interpret present experiences. In a sense, the memory function is the background color on which we paint the daily experiences of our life. Personal history, culture, gender and genetic history all play a role in shaping this function. For instance, if you were born in America, you see reality from the point of view of an American. If you are a white male, you interpret reality from the perspective of a white male. If you are a black female, your view of reality is influenced by this background.

The sensory function draws upon past experiences as it creates our personal, unique sense of reality. When ten people are in a room, they bring with them ten different views of reality determined by ten different personal histories and ten different sensory minds creating that reality. If the ten people grew up in the same culture and share the same beliefs and values, they will generally agree on many things and similarly interpret actions and communications that occur in the room. But people who have different beliefs and values may not only disagree on the meaning of what happens in the room, but may actually also describe the events differently. Each individual will see and interpret the events from his or her own perspective, and that personal perspective is reality for each individual. Two people having the same experience will each see and interpret that experience in a unique, individual way, and they may not always agree on what really happened.

Personal reality begins with perception, in which the creative force of the mind organizes and interprets sensory data to build a meaningful picture of the world. A single act of perception involves a complex mixture of past experiences (memory), beliefs, values and expectations. Even our constitution, genes, stress levels, and health shape and color our perceptions and influence not only what we see, but also how we feel, think and act.

Language plays a key role in how we define the reality we experience. When we talk about something being good or bad, exciting or dull, wonderful or awful, we are not describing the objective reality itself, but rather our perceptions of it. Our sense of personal reality is determined more by our mental/emotional reactions, our thoughts and feelings about the event, than the event itself. In other words, it is not so much *what* happens to us as what those events *mean* to us. And it is the words we use that create the meaning. Each word we use has some emotional connection in the unconscious mind, either positive or negative, and sometimes both. As we think about things, we unwittingly create our own misery. We aren't aware of the power and impact that our choice of language has on our emotions.

For example, the moment I start thinking about how much I miss a distant friend, and what fun we could be having now, I begin to feel bad. The more I think about how things *could* be, the more miserable I become. Popular songs are forever rehashing these emotions. Just look at the words of a country-western song about missing someone. Even if you don't feel bad when you begin singing it, by the end of the song you will! The words are designed to evoke a feeling of loneliness. The more you sing the song, the more you repeat the words, the more miserable you will feel.

The language we use directly leads to the emotions we feel. Emotions are powerful and positive resources. They tell us when we are in harmony with life and when we aren't. Emotions stimulate, challenge and motivate us to accomplish what we want. Passion and inspiration help us achieve great things in life and create wonderful relationships. Without emotions, life is empty and meaningless. Emotions are essential to living a full human life, but we must learn how to direct and use emotional energy intelligently and skillfully.

Unfortunately, without intending to, most of us become victimized by our own emotions. They distort perceptions, interfere with thinking and even create disease when negatively channeled. We often blame others for our emotional reactions, whether they are good or bad. We say things like "You make me mad!" or "You make me feel good!" Both statements are false. Our emotional reactions are totally our own creation. Although we certainly can't control what someone else does, we absolutely have the power to control our reactions to what they do. We may not have the skill to control our reactions, but that doesn't change the fact that we determine them ourselves. No one else stimulates our endocrine system, and no one else directs our brain functions.

Though it can be hard to accept this simple fact, the anxieties of loneliness are self-created. No one makes us feel alone and abandoned—we do that to ourselves. That doesn't mean that we should blame ourselves any more than we should blame others. Certainly we don't do this to ourselves intentionally. No one wants to feel left out, isolated, alone and miserable. We create these emotional reactions because we lack self-knowledge. Because we don't know who we are or how the mind works, we lack the skill we need to take control of our thoughts and emotions.

We solidify these emotional reactions through the fourth activity of the sensory mind, the power of habit. Our emotions and language use are controlled by habits. Instead of choosing to think or feel a certain way, we act out of habit. That's why we always talk about *emotional reactions* instead of *emotional choices*. By the time we feel an emotional reaction, we are already disturbed by it. It becomes increasingly difficult to redirect the emotional energy into more useful channels.

Habits are one of the most powerful tools of the mind. They regulate every part of life, from the most trivial, such as which leg we put first into a pair of pants, to the most profound, such as the way we think about and solve problems. Our patterns of thought, the language we use, even the way we go about facing challenges, are regulated by habit. Every skill we have is based on habit, whether they are the skills of a neurosurgeon, a baseball player or a carpenter. The more we repeat (practice) any activity, the more skillful we become. Whenever we feel lonely, unknowingly we are practicing feeling lonely. The more often we do this, the more skilled we become at loneliness.

We don't realize that we are practicing something so negative. We focus only on how badly we feel, not on how the feeling was created. So instead of making a conscious choice—do I want to feel lonely and miserable now, or not—we allow the well-practiced habit of feeling lonely and miserable to take over. Once the habit of thinking and feeling a certain way is established, it becomes an automatic response to a particular set of circumstances. The more often we feel lonely and depressed, the stronger the habit becomes, and the more often we will feel that way.

Both positive and negative emotional reactions become habits. For example, if I grow up believing that I can succeed no matter what the challenge, then I face the world with confidence, accept change as an opportunity, and think clearly and creatively about problems. Every day I practice being confident and creative. After a while, I will become quite skilled at it. However, if I grow up believing that I am not very competent, then I face the world fearfully, react to change as a threat, become inflexible and uncreative and lack the ability to think clearly about the problems I face. Every day I practice being fearful, inflexible and uncreative. After a while, I will become quite skilled at it.

Most of us grow up with habits we didn't consciously choose for ourselves. We are taught from an early age that unless we are popular, unless people think well of us and like us, unless we have someone to love us, we aren't valuable. We learn to define our importance by what others think of us. An entire life can be spent worrying about what the neighbors think. If and when we "fall in love" with someone, then we are really in trouble. If that person doesn't return this love, we feel worthless. Such misery and anxieties arise out of misdirected thoughts, beliefs and habits of the mind.

Few of us grow up without developing negative habits, fear and self-hatred. If we are unaware of their sources, then we cannot counteract their influence. It is tragic to spend a whole life being controlled by the habits that take root by happenstance rather than by choice. The world doesn't keep us from being successful, happy and fulfilled; rather, it is the patterns and habits of the mind that do so. No matter how many people love me, as long as I continue to act on the negative habits in my mind, I will be lonely.

These four activities of the sensory mind interact to create our personal sense of reality. As long as we remain unaware of their dynamics, we unknowingly create mind-stuff that leads to dependency, emotional problems and loneliness. This ignorance causes us to remain isolated from ourselves, lacking the knowledge and skill necessary to direct powerful resources of the mind. But growth in self-knowledge enables us to harness the mind to create happiness and fulfillment.

Feeling good is not an accident. It results when a healthy, skillful mind is guided by self-awareness and self-control.

TECHNIQUES TO CONTROL EMOTIONAL REACTIONS

We can take control and direct the sensory and memory functions to create habits that produce joy instead of anxiety, contentment instead of unhappiness and restlessness. It is a simple, but not necessarily easy, task to create and maintain a powerful, peaceful mind that functions smoothly whether or not we have lovers and friends. The first step is to take control of emotional reactions. By training ourselves in effective stress management techniques—diaphragmatic breathing, deep relaxation and emotional control—we can reduce the chronic stress and tension that feed emotional imbalance.

The first two basic skills, diaphragmatic breathing and deep relaxation, are absolutely necessary for reducing chronic stress and tension. Both are easy to learn. Diaphragmatic breathing balances the autonomic nervous system, eliminating and preventing stress; deep relaxation reduces chronic tension in the body, allowing you to work in a more relaxed fashion. Both are practiced using the relaxation posture described below.

THE RELAXATION POSTURE

Lie on your back on a pad or a carpeted floor and gently close your eyes. Place your feet a comfortable distance apart, about twelve to eighteen inches, and your arms and hands slightly away from the body, palms facing up and fingers gently curled. Use a small pillow or a folded blanket under your head to support the curve of your neck. Do not place the limbs too far apart. Lie in a symmetrical position. In this posture the body lies still and relaxed. It is important to avoid drowsiness; keep the mind alert and focused on the flow of the breath.

Diaphragmatic breathing is the natural way for humans to breathe under normal circumstances. For instance, if you watch an infant breathe, you will never see the chest moving—only the stomach moving up and down as if there were a small pump in the stomach. Unfortunately, by the time most people have finished high school, they breathe using the chest muscles instead of the diaphragm. Chest breathing is the body's emergency breathing mechanism. When you breathe with the chest, you create a subtle but chronic fight-or-flight reaction in the body, which leads to chronic stress and tension. This unnecessary stress is the root cause of many illnesses, including heart disease. When you breathe with the diaphragm, the motion leads to autonomic balance and prevention of stress.

Fortunately, it takes very little effort to reestablish diaphragmatic breathing as your moment-to-moment breathing habit. Simply practice diaphragmatic breathing for ten to fifteen minutes before going to sleep and when you wake up in the morning. Gradually, the easy, rhythmic motion of diaphragmatic breathing will replace the strained, unnatural chest breathing. The more often you practice diaphragmatic breathing during the day, the more quickly the old habit will change.

When you practice diaphragmatic breathing, concentrate on making the breath very smooth and even. The inhalation and exhalation should be of the same length, and you should maintain the same flow pressure throughout the entire breath. Eliminate all pauses, stops and shakiness in the breath. Imagine the breath as a wheel or circle moving evenly and smoothly through the body. The more smooth and even the breath, the more balanced the autonomic nervous system will become and the more relaxed you will be. The specific instructions, given below, will help you reestablish diaphragmatic breathing and eliminate stress. For a more detailed explanation of the relationship between breathing and stress, read *The Quest for Personal Power* by the author.

THE PRACTICE OF DIAPHRAGMATIC BREATHING

Diaphragmatic breathing is so important that it must be considered the foundation of all self-mastery skills. It helps create a healthy body and develop the power of our mind. There are three key points about diaphragmatic breathing:

1. **Efficiency:** The primary purpose of breathing is to provide oxygen to the bloodstream. The diaphragm is designed by nature to utilize the natural efficiency of our respiratory system. Proper diaphragmatic breathing will minimize pressure on the cardiovascular system and help prevent essential hypertension.

2. **Neural Connections:** The direct relationship between breathing, the autonomic nervous system and our emotions provides a mechanism to control both stress in the body and emotional reactions in the mind. By taking control of the way we breathe, we take control of the autonomic nervous system. This gives us the power to control the fight-or-flight and possum alarm reactions.

3. **Nose Breathing:** The nose serves as a switchboard for the entire nervous system. Breathing through the mouth alters neural patterning and can lead to greater physical weakness and even dangerous health conditions.

TO PRACTICE: To reestablish diaphragmatic breathing as your moment-to-moment breathing pattern, you must practice for a minimum of ten to fifteen minutes twice a day. (The easiest time to practice is when you go to bed and when you first wake up in the morning. This will help you have a restful sleep.)

Assume the relaxation posture discussed on page 26.

Place your right hand on your stomach with your little finger over the navel and the other fingers stretching up toward your chest. Place your left hand on the upper part of your chest with the little finger between the two breasts. When the diaphragm contracts, it flattens out and pushes against the internal organs in the abdominal cavity. Instead of the chest going up and down, the stomach moves out and in as if there were a small balloon inside. Now breathe as if you are filling this small balloon in your stomach. Your stomach and right hand will rise with the inhalation and fall with the exhalation. This should be very gentle—no effort or work is required. Don't try to completely fill or empty your lungs. Let your body decide how much air it needs. There should be no movement at all in the left hand. You should feel a slight motion in the lower portion of the chest cavity, but the upper portion should remain still.

Within a few moments you will feel more rested and quiet. Do not try to force the breath. Notice how easy it is to breathe deeply and easily without any effort. Practice being an observer, allowing the body to do the breathing for you.

To build a stronger diaphragmatic response, place an eight to ten pound pliable weight, such as a wrist weight, a sand bag or a sack of beans or rice across the upper abdomen when you practice. This weight-lifting strengthens the diaphragm and establishes diaphragmatic breathing more quickly.

You can speed the process by being aware of your breathing pattern as much as possible during the day. The more often you correct it, the faster you will replace your old habit of chest breathing with diaphragmatic breathing.

Deep relaxation can be easily learned by using a good relaxation technique. Probably the best way to learn deep relaxation is to buy an audiocassette tape of relaxation exercises and practice every day. When you do a deep relaxation exercise, be sure to lie in the relaxation posture and focus on the exercise. Don't allow yourself to fall asleep. When you learn how to become completely relaxed while remaining fully alert, you'll be well on your way to developing the skill of deep relaxation.

The most common relaxation techniques involve imagery, auto-hypnosis or suggestion. To practice, lie in the relaxation posture and imagine that your muscles feel very warm and heavy. This reduces structural tension. One of the most simple relaxation techniques is to close your eyes and picture your forehead becoming very smooth and even. Allow the smoothness to pass down the face, through the eye-brows, cheeks, corners of the mouth, even relaxing the lower jaws and ears. With practice, this visualization technique can lead to a fairly relaxed state. A more effective approach is to use the breath. Two simple relaxation techniques, "2:1 breathing" and the "sweeping breath" exercise, are given below.

2:1 BREATHING

Practice diaphragmatic breathing until your breathing is balanced and even and very smooth. Then, gently slow the rate of exhalation until you are breathing out for about as twice as long as you are inhaling. (It might be necessary to slightly shorten the inhalation.) You are simply changing the rhythm of the breath. Don't worry about filling or emptying the lungs. The purpose is to alter the motion of the lungs in a systematic way. You may count to six on the exhalation and three on the inhalation, or eight on the exhalation and four on the inhalation—whatever is most comfortable for you. After establishing this gentle rhythm, stop the mental counting and focus on the smoothness and evenness of the breath flow. Eliminate all jerks and pauses. Maintain 2:1 diaphragmatic breathing for as long as you wish. Pay attention to what happens to your heartbeat and any other changes in your body.

THE SWEEPING BREATH

Begin by lying in the relaxation posture. Breathe with the diaphragm, allowing your breath to become very even and smooth.

Now visualize the body as a hollow reed. Then breathe in as if inhaling through the toes and filling the body with breath to the crown of the head. Exhale as if you are breathing back down through the body and out the toes. Breathe easily and gently without any effort. Let your body decide how much air you need.

Concentrate on feeling the entire body breathe and imagine every cell and pore in your body breathing in and out. It's as if you are feeling your entire body expanding on the inhalation and contracting on the exhalation.

After a few moments, visualize the breath on the inhalation as a wave washing upon the shore and on the exhalation, receding back into the sea. Maintain this image for as long as you wish.

The most effective technique to control emotional reactions is to control "mind-chatter" by using breath awareness. Pay attention to your mind—notice how you are constantly talking to yourself? We call that thinking, but that is a very generous term. Most of the time little real thought is going on. We are simply talking to ourselves, answering ourselves, even talking to others and having them answer us. All of this takes place inside the head.

This ongoing flow of mind-chatter reflects the creative force of the mind. This powerful force can be used in positive or negative ways.

When we worry, we constantly remind ourselves of terrible things that *might* happen. Our focus of attention is not on what is happening now, but what might happen in the future. This anticipation of harm creates the destructive emotional reaction called fear, one of two dragons that live in the sensory mind. Fear doesn't exist in the present, it is a fantasy of some future possibility. We never fear what is happening, only what might happen.

The body's reaction to fear is the "fight-or-flight" alarm reaction. The popular myth is that this alarm reaction is helpful. We are told by the experts that this is a protective mechanism, but in truth, it is nothing more than the consequence of a fearful mind. We get uptight and anxious, and we overutilize our energy, leading directly to fatigue and burn-out. While the fight-or-flight reaction is somewhat helpful, we pay an enormous price—stress, disease, anxiety, unhappiness, even burn-out. As we shall see later, fear and its physical expression, the fight-or-flight reaction, is the product of an untrained mind. We do not need fear and the fight-or-flight reaction to protect ourselves, act effectively in emergency situations or overcome challenges.

Anticipating future fantasies of harm is not the only way we create disturbances with mind-chatter. Unfortunately, when no one else is attacking us, we often attack ourselves. We become judgmental, we remember all the *stupid* mistakes we have made and we dwell on how things never seem to go right. This sort of mind-chatter creates self-hatred, the second dragon of the sensory mind. The body's reaction to self-hatred is known as the "possum response," which de-energizes us and makes us feel depressed and defeated. This alarm reaction, seldom recognized by most stress experts, creates just as much disease and unhappiness as the fight-or-flight reaction. When preoccupied with the mistakes, failures and terrible experiences of the past, our minds create this depressed emotional disturbance.

Mind-chatter can also fuel our loneliness. We begin talking to ourselves about how lonely we are and how nice it would be if we had someone near us. The more we think about it, the more lonely we feel and the more emotionally disturbed we become. We may become depressed, we may feel anxious or we may experience both at the same time. We are very creative in finding ways to make ourselves miserable.

However, the moment we stop thinking about how terrible things are and focus on solutions to the problem, the emotional reaction calms. Often we cannot control the events around us, but we can use a technique called "breath awareness" to take control of our mind-chatter. Begin by observing your mind for a moment. Don't get involved with the thinking; just witness the thoughts as they pass through your awareness. Now focus your attention on the *feeling* of the breath as it passes in and out of your nostrils. When you inhale, you will feel a slight touch of coolness at the opening of the nostrils. When you exhale, you will feel a very subtle touch of warmth. It may be difficult to feel the warmth at first, but you will feel the movement of the air as it passes out of the nostrils.

Don't *think* about the breath, but concentrate on *feeling* the breath—a slight touch of coolness when you breathe in, a very subtle touch of warmth when you breathe out. Be aware of what happens to your thoughts, your breath and the inside of your body when you focus on the breath. You will notice four things:

1. The chatter in your mind stops, and your mind becomes clear and calm.

2. Your breathing slows and becomes more stable.

3. You feel a slight release as your body relaxes. (Mind-chatter no longer makes demands for physical action. The body's natural condition is relaxation. The more focused, calm and quiet the mind, the more relaxed your body becomes.)

4. Feelings of loneliness, anxiety and depression disappear.

You may have to rely on breath awareness many times during the day to clear your mind and refocus your attention. The more you use the technique, the more skilled you will become. After a little practice you will build the habit of clearing your mind instead of allowing it to chatter on and on about how lonely, isolated and unhappy you are. This frees you from the anxieties of loneliness. Once this mental clarity becomes a habit, you will spend little time feeling isolated, lonely and depressed.

But dealing with the anxieties of loneliness isn't the same as solving the fundamental problem of loneliness. These first steps, diaphragmatic breathing, deep relaxation and breath awareness, are just the beginning of the journey. These powerful tools help control the emotions, freeing up energy to explore the deeper levels of the mind. The next step involves tapping the third function of the mind, discrimination.

THE DISCRIMINATING FUNCTION:
INTELLECT AND WISDOM

Deep within every mind lies the pure intellect—the capacity to know truth, to understand life as it really is, not as our habits dictate. Through discrimination, we discern the cause-effect relationships that constitute actual reality. With this power we develop the capacity to distinguish between what is real and what our fears and desires cause us to see. In other words, we can go beyond emotional, mental and physical habits, beyond illusions, and see the truth, including the nature of loneliness.

This is an awesome capacity. We don't have to be a slave to our habits. We can make decisions based on insight and wisdom rather than emotional reactions and unexamined beliefs. We don't have to act out of fear, anxiety or self-hatred, nor do we have to be fooled by illusions. Through discrimination, the mind evaluates information and impressions, makes decisions and judgments and creates knowledge. We have the power to analyze a situation and respond effectively. But if unhealthy habits dominate us, so will illusions.

In its pure form, the intellect generates intuitive knowledge and insight that allows us to see the real consequences of actions we are considering or taking in the present. This inner wisdom helps us make the right choices, avoiding later regret and guilt. We have all experienced this. Think of a time when you wanted to do something, but right before you did it, a small, quiet voice inside your head said, "Better not do that." You paused for a moment, but desire, fear or anxiety took control and you went ahead and did it anyhow. Several days (or months or years) later, when it becomes all-too-apparent that you made the wrong choice, you say, "I knew I shouldn't have done that." How many times have you heard someone say, "I knew I shouldn't have gotten involved in this relationship"?

Illusions cannot fool the pure intellect. They are limited to the superficial levels of the personality and gain their strength only through the perceptions, language, emotions and habits of the sensory function. But the discrimination function is very subtle and quiet. Therefore, the noisy, active sensory function can easily bury the softer voice of discrimination. Distracted by desires and fears and locked into the habits of the mind, we often find it difficult to access that still, quiet voice. The more disturbance we create, the more difficult it becomes to discern the subtle cause-effect relationships in our choices and actions.

We can tune into the wisdom of the discriminating function by developing a deeply calm and quiet mind. Concentration and meditation open the door to this level of self-mastery. (Meditation is discussed in chapter 4.) Once we attain the ability to discriminate, we break free of the illusions and come face-to-face with the dragon and see loneliness for what it truly is.

THE EGO FUNCTION: HOME OF THE DRAGON

The ego, the fourth function of the mind, coordinates all other functions and activities. The task of the ego is to create an identity center, to define what is part of the personality and what is not. The ego acts as the general manager of the personality, allowing us to act and experience life as unique, separate individuals. It creates a sense of separateness that distinguishes the individual mind from the rest of the world and defines what constitutes "I-ness." It produces the experience of subjectivity. When sensory impressions come into the mind, the ego transforms them into a personal experience by relating them to an individual identity. Thus, through the sensory function, music is heard, but the ego adds its influence to declare, "I hear music."

The ego limits the sense of I-ness to its own realm, one particular mind/body/behavior complex. The experience of being a separate entity is created by the ego. You are obviously separate from me. You have your own body, thoughts and actions, and I have my own body, thoughts and actions. You may feel the same emotions, but you can't feel *my* emotions. You may think the same thoughts, but you don't think *my* thoughts. We are each different, even though we share the same room, the same culture, the same thoughts, the same feelings, even the same experiences. But you don't experience what I experience, and I don't experience what you experience.

The ego often gets a bad rap, but it serves a critical function. Unless ego creates a center of identity, a sense of unique individuality, we cannot function effectively. A person whose ego does not function may end up in a mental hospital, unable to piece together a coherent, workable reality for life. Weak egos lead to personal problems such as insecurity, anxiety and depression. We must constantly deal with the problems created by weak egos at work, at home, in our communities and in politics at all levels—local, national and international. When egos are weak, "I" becomes very important. We all know individuals who are very successful in one part of life—sports heroes, movie stars, executives, entrepreneurs—but are real jerks in interpersonal relationships. When people consider themselves overly-important and need to prove it, they strut their stuff to make others feel less important. People with weak egos often gossip and attack others. This only reinforces separateness from others and leads to even greater loneliness. As the lives of many famous and wealthy people clearly show, fame and fortune are no insurance against loneliness.

A healthy, strong ego is essential to a healthy, successful life. By coordinating all the different functions of the mind, the ego creates a powerful tool, the personality, for the purpose of effectively serving the needs of the individual. A strong ego is characterized by love, inner strength (self-confidence) and gentleness. Unfortunately, it is easy to confuse having a strong ego with having a big ego. Having a big ego inevitably means being self-centered, impressed with one's own importance and hell-bent to get one's own way. These are symptoms of a weak ego, not a strong, healthy one. Strong egos have no need to dominate others. They are expansive in their relationships—capable of giving and sharing—open to new ideas and able to learn from others.

BUILDING A HEALTHY EGO THROUGH LOVE

The foundation for a healthy, strong ego is the love we receive as children. Infants need to be loved and held or else they will die. The first five or six years of life is the critical time for developing the ego, the sense of I-ness that defines the individual personality. The greatest need for the child is the loving attention of the parents and community. Without it, the child develops unhealthy and destructive patterns that will cripple the adult personality. When the parents are selfish, the child learns to be selfish. When the parents are cold and distant, the child feels unloved and learns to be unlovable or becomes dependent on attention.

Violence in any form—emotional, verbal or physical—distorts the development of the child's ego and harms the mind of the child. During the first five to seven years of life, a child should never, never be struck. Striking a child never benefits the child. It is always destructive to the sensitive, developing mind of the child. Violence of any kind is a clear indication that the adult, not the child, is out of control. A child needs limits that are firm, clear and consistent. But if these limits are not applied with love, understanding and gentleness, then the delicate formation of the ego function is harmed. The belief that "to spare the rod is to spoil the child" is nothing more than sheer ignorance. There is *no excuse* for violence against any child. The distortions created by violence during childhood become the emotional disturbances and problems that we face as adults.

Simply put, the more love we receive as children, the healthier we become as adults. We never outgrow the human need for love. It nurtures the development and health of the personality. As we grow into strong individuals, free from petty fears, anxieties and self-hatred, we can easily satisfy this need through marriage and close relationships with family and friends.

An individual with a strong, healthy ego can expand the sense of self to include family, loved ones, friends and others. He or she doesn't limit himself or herself to the identity of mind and body, but can include an ever-increasing circle of others. He or she can feel compassion even for people living in a different part of the world. The healthier and stronger the ego, the more the individual can expand the limits imposed by the ego function.

People with weak egos create increasingly rigid, limiting boundaries of identification. Their sense of self becomes smaller and weaker, increasingly threatened by the world outside of themselves. The weaker the ego, the more limited the identity, and the greater the suffering is. For instance, one of the easiest ways to measure neurosis and unhappiness is to count the number of times an individual says "I," "me," or "mine" in a conversation. The more self-centered an individual is, the smaller their sense of self, the more rigid their belief systems and the greater their isolation, loneliness and unhappiness.

Creating the experience of unique individuality is the necessary work of the ego function. It is also the source of loneliness. Loneliness is powerful because it involves the most crucial issue of all—the experience of personal identity. The realization of our own separateness is the root cause of loneliness. And since every human has an ego, every human experiences being a separate, unique individual, and every human suffers loneliness. And if we view ourselves simply as the mind/body complex, this is the end of the line.

We all grow up with weaknesses in the ego structure, but through self-knowledge and self-discipline, we can minimize those weaknesses and increase our strengths. But in the end, even strong, healthy egos feel the isolation of individuality and experience loneliness. We must find a way to transcend the ego, to go beyond the limitations of this powerful function of the mind. We must experience an identity that is not limited by mind and body or by the emotional attachments we have for others.

SLAYING THE DRAGON: THE END OF LONELINESS

The answer to loneliness is love, but not the love we receive from others. The love we receive from others is absolutely necessary for the ego-self, but not the spiritual Self. Loneliness has nothing to do with other people or their love. It is the people we love and who love us that make us feel lonely. We never miss our enemies. We don't feel lonely when we think about people whom we don't like. We only miss the ones we care for. So how can getting more people to love us do anything but make us more lonely?

We feel isolated and alone because we aren't sharing our love with those around us. *It is not the love we receive, but the love we give, that frees us from loneliness and isolation.* We can search the world for the perfect partner, we can have countless lovers and friends and we can receive love without end. But unless we ourselves express love, we will never be free from loneliness.

The love we desperately seek flows from the very core of our being. This is not the self-love that psychologists talk about. It has to do with becoming love itself. This is the expression, and the power, of the spiritual Self. As long as we remain unaware of and neglect this spiritual Self, we will feel lonely and isolated.

Loneliness is, in essence, a spiritual problem. When we are isolated from the spiritual Self we experience loneliness. We compensate by finding lovers and friends, and we develop philosophical insights and religious beliefs and faith to fill the emptiness. But we cannot put an end to loneliness until we touch the power of our human core, the spiritual Self.

Human beings are not the sum total of the physical sensations of the body, the thoughts and beliefs of the intellect or the ups and downs of emotional reactions. Our real identity is spiritual. We confuse the tool (the personality and all its resources) with the owner, the spiritual Self. As long as we remain unaware of this Truth within ourselves, we know ourselves only as the ego-self. Consequently, we confuse love with emotional attachment. We fear death and change because they pose threats to the ego. We feel loneliness because we falsely believe that our separateness is the ultimate truth about us. To resolve loneliness, to be fearless in the face of death and change, to touch the power and wisdom of the Divine, we must reach beyond the limitations of the human personality to the spiritual core, the mystical, infinite Self that is the same, universal Self in all others.

So let us continue our journey to the spiritual Self. It requires stillness instead of movement, unlearning instead of learning. The next step is to see how the pure love of the spiritual Self is clouded and colored by the ego-self and to free ourselves from the illusion we mistakenly call love. We will discover how to reach beyond the small ego-self, with its beliefs, emotions, needs, desires and fears, and experience a Self that has no limits, boundaries, or isolation. And at our journey's end, we will experience the flame of pure love and free ourselves from the curse of loneliness.

CHAPTER 3

LOVE AND ILLUSION: SPIRIT AND EGO

Attachment creates bondage and love gives freedom.
Don't confuse yourself by mistaking attachment for love.

DID YOU EVER WONDER where love comes from? Love is the most ancient of travelers. The ultimate and only reality, love is the endless, eternal face of the Divine. Love is pure, a flame without smoke. But what we often call love is clouded and colored by the smoke of emotional dependency. The wants, needs, desires and even fears of the ego color and distort the purity of love, and we end up with emotions and feelings that are painful and destructive. The ego, with its emphasis on *I, me* and *mine,* turns the joy and freedom that characterize pure love into emotional dependency, creating the anxiety of loneliness. And the more we chase this illusionary type of love, the more lonely we become.

When we say we love someone, what we often mean is that this person satisfies our needs and fulfills our desires. He or she makes us feel good, safe, secure and happy. Naturally, we become emotionally attached to this special person and we try to make the relationship secure. Because the relationship has been built on our own needs, we expect the person to behave in a certain way, we question their motives and behavior when they act differently, and we feel jealous and insecure if they pay attention to someone else. Love becomes possessive, restrictive and demanding. We want to own what we love, and when we do so, we no longer love what we own.

The word "love" takes on the coloration of our emotional needs and wants. The term itself takes on so many meanings—even conflicting ones—and we become confused about what it really means. We use love to describe feelings of attraction, passion, lust and sensuality. It can also denote the highest form of selflessness. We love the play we just saw, we love the new car we just bought, we love those who agree with our beliefs (and hate those who think differently), and we love abstract ideals such as world peace and justice. Politicians love us when they want our vote, salesmen love us when they want our money, and our parents love us when we do something the whole community applauds. When someone tells us they love us, we don't know what the person really feels: love, envy, superficial social friendliness or the desire to manipulate us in some way.

We all know the heartache and disappointment created when a lover finds someone new to love. How many times have you heard someone say, "Love hurts"? Some of our greatest literature stems from this pain, but is this really love? The real subject is the emotional traumas of loss, desire, needs and wants. Everything is focused on what *I* want, what *I* miss and need, how *I* feel. When the other person is mentioned, it is only in relationship to how happy or unhappy this person makes *me*. This is about emotional dependency, the suffering and loss of an individual ego. What kind of love is this?

Love is often another word for control. The people we love must behave in a certain way or we won't love them anymore. We use guilt, we withhold affection, and we even bargain for love exchanging favors. The force of emotional dependency can be so strong that many stay in destructive and abusive relationships and still call it love. The man who beats his wife claims he loves her, but the truth is horrendously different. This is evident in the response given by O. J. Simpson to a question about the accusation that he killed his ex-wife, Nicole Brown Simpson: "Even if I did do this, it would have to have been because I loved her very much, right?" Though he was later acquitted of the crime in a very controversial decision, this attitude is tragically characteristic of men who abuse their wives and lovers.

In our ignorance we even make God's love conditional. If we don't "do the right thing," have the right beliefs, repent in time, then that same loving God is going to condemn us to eternal damnation. Again, we have to ask, what kind of love is this? What kind of loving God gives freedom of choice and then demands you make the right choice, or else! Religions that trade on fear, guilt and punishment are destructive to the human mind, make a mockery of God and have little to do with love.

What we call love is often nothing more than smoke and mirrors, reflecting our own confusion and egocentric needs, fears and wants. Cindy, an attractive woman who loves to fall in love, is a classic example of love-confusion. She complains that her relationships never seem to last more than nine or ten months. For some reason, she never seems to find someone who fits her real needs. When she first starts a relationship, the guy seems to be perfect. But over time, as the relationship deepens, she always finds something to dislike. "Why can't I see the real person before I spend so much time on the relationship?" she wants to know. What Cindy really likes is the excitement and attention she gets from a new lover. As the relationship progresses, and the newness wears away, she begins to get bored. Instead of taking the time to build depth in the relationship, which calls for her to give more of herself, she demands more and more attention. This, of course, puts pressures on the relationship and leads to unpleasant feelings for both parties. Finally, she finds someone new to feed her need for attention. She explains this pattern as a tendency to fall in love with the wrong guy. This excuse allows her to continue the same pattern in the next relationship rather than getting to the heart of the problem.

Cindy doesn't fall into love, but into her own emotional needs. She needs attention in order to feel good about herself. She isn't intentionally misleading anyone, but she constantly misleads herself. She is stuck in her emotional habits. Calling her dependency and need for attention "love" only confuses and complicates the problem. As long as she maintains her illusion about love, she will continue to be unhappy, confused and lonely.

Like Cindy, most of us have suffered from love-confusion. We confuse love with the wants, needs and fears of the ego-self, and in so doing, we set the stage for loneliness, despair and unhappiness. The more we focus on how *I* feel, what *I* need, or what's in it for *me*, the less we experience the pure flame of love. The greater our egocentricity, the more self-concern we have, the more we experience the anxiety of loneliness.

THE POWER OF PURE LOVE

And yet, we experience times when love makes life so sublime, so perfect, so complete that nothing else seems to matter. It happens when we "fall in love," and suddenly the whole world becomes light and wonderful. It happens when we take part in the birth of a child and feel the full power of love streaming out of us toward that new life. Even the most hardened cynic is affected by the innocence of love and power of that event. Deep in our core, we know that, in spite of our disappointments and loneliness, love—the real thing—can heal us. It gives us the power to do the impossible, to make changes that will positively transform our own lives and those of others.

Barry would never consider himself a great human being. A non-drinking alcoholic and Alcoholics Anonymous sponsor, he was trying to rebuild his career. Divorced from his wife when his son was three, he was pretty much an absent father. His great sadness was his failure as a father, which meant to him that he was also a failure as a human being. Then, Barry faced circumstances that seemed to point to almost certain tragedy. His son, Sean, growing up in Chicago, had become involved with gangs. By the time he was a junior in high school, Sean was in deep trouble: kicked out of school, arrested for several major felonies, and facing serious jail time. At this crisis point, Barry reached into himself and, moved by the power of love, transformed his son's life as well as his own.

When he heard of his son's arrest and pending trial, something happened inside Barry. His worries and concerns for himself disappeared. What was important was his son's life. He *had* to act. Barry flew to Chicago and, moving as quickly as the law and his own legs would carry him, completed the procedures necessary to take legal custody of his son. He arrived at his son's trial with the freshly-signed custody papers in his hand. His son had no idea that his father was in town.

Addressing the judge, Barry said, "Your Honor, I now have legal custody of my son. If the court will assign my son over to me, I promise the court that I will take him to Seattle, away from the gang he runs with, and he will finish school and stay out of trouble. But you have to decide now, Your Honor, because my plane is leaving in forty minutes."

His son had no warning that this was going to happen and was instantly hostile to the idea. Jumping up, he said, "There's no way I'm going with him!"

Addressing the judge, Barry said, "Would you give me a moment to speak to my son? What I am about to say is not directed to the court, but only to my son."

When the judge agreed, Barry turned to his son and, with great intensity, said, "Shut the f— up! You will either go to prison or with me. You don't have any other choices. So just sit down and keep your big mouth shut!"

Turning back to the judge, Barry said, "Excuse me, Your Honor, but this was not directed to the court."

Before Barry had finished his sentence, the judge brought down the gavel and granted Barry full custody of his son. Both Barry and his son caught the plane to Seattle.

By the time they arrived in Seattle, Barry's son was furious. Barry said to him, "I know I'm not a father—I've failed at that role. But I sure can be your sponsor. You are not out of control with alcohol like I was, but you are out of control with life and with gangs. I'm going to see to it that you gain back your control."

It wasn't easy for either of them. But in a year and a half, Sean finished high school and began work on a college degree. He has since earned an associate's degree in law enforcement and is now completing a bachelor's degree program in law enforcement.

When Barry brought Sean back to Chicago to start college, Sean first wanted to visit the dean of the high school that threw him out. Sean walked into the dean's office and showed him his graduation certificate and college enrollment papers.

The dean was not only surprised, but very impressed. "I was certain that you were either dead or locked up by now!" he stated. "How were you able to get free from the gangs and the trouble that you were in?"

Sean replied, "It was tough, but I had a spiritual awakening, and that made the difference."

The dean asked, "A spiritual awakening? Do you remember when that happened?"

"Yes," Sean replied. "I remember very clearly. It was the second day in Seattle. I told my dad that I was leaving and started out the door. I didn't think a fat old man could move so fast. My spiritual awakening happened somewhere in the middle of my being spun around on my back over my father's head and being forcibly redirected away from the door, and away from my past life! I knew then that I had to straighten myself out, and that my father would do everything in his power to help me."

Barry committed everything to helping his son save his life and, in doing so, overcame the dragons in his own life. In his act of love for his son, Barry became the father that he always wanted to be. Through the power of love, Barry reached greatness within himself.

Acts of greatness are acts of pure love, the expression of the spiritual Self. They are seldom as dramatic as Barry's, but they are always powerful and life-transforming, and they free us from fears and worries. Acts of pure love take many forms, but they always have one significant characteristic: they completely lack egocentric thought or action. In other words, the sense of individuality, the sense that *I* am doing this, or *I* am receiving this, completely disappears. This loss of egocentric focus is the defining quality of pure love. It is a totally outward-flowing, irresistible expression of inner strength, compassion and joy.

Through these acts, we discover the power of the pure love of our spiritual core, and we are able to be more joyful more successful as human beings. Regardless of when and how these acts happen, we never forget them or the effect they have on us and others. They inspire us to greater effort, to greater community, to greater joy. This is the real gift of love: it transforms our personalities through the power of the spiritual Self, and we know beyond a shadow of a doubt that we are no longer alone.

Unfortunately, our personal experience is not always freeing, empowering, unlimiting and unlimited. We have tantalizing glimpses. We are inspired by examples, but for the most part, we seldom realize the power and beauty of love. For example, the love of family and children certainly seem to express pure love. But even here, the ego-self often asserts its dominance. The vast majority of us love our children and willingly give time, limit our careers, give up comforts and work to create security for them. We don't even think of this as a sacrifice. Our only desire is to do the best for children. But notice, we do this for *our* children, but do we ensure the well-being of all children? Of course not, they are other people's responsibility. We will express concern, but they are not *our* children.

The word *our* defines the way we relate to, and care for, children. This is the power of the ego-self. It is the ego that says that this is *my* child, and this child is *not* my child. Even in the love of family, ego asserts itself.

Pure love makes no distinction. Christ was the embodiment of the spiritual Self. He showed, by his own example, the unconditional nature of the pure love. Christ said, "Suffer the little children to come unto me." He didn't say, "Suffer only the little Jewish children to come unto me," or ask only for his nephews and nieces or just those children from his village. In example after example, Christ extended this love to those who were demeaned or scorned by society. He was never concerned about his own needs, only for the needs of those whom he served. Christ loved all children, all people, equally. This unlimited love is the great example of the Christ.

Ego-self always makes a distinction. It is controlled by its own natural needs, desires, fears and worries. Ego-self defines love by what satisfies, pleasures and makes the ego-self feel secure, happy and content. Its love is self-serving, and thus, by its very nature, it creates separation and isolation. Emotional attachment feeds loneliness by reinforcing the sense of individual identity and holding it up as the ultimate reality.

THE FOUR NATURAL DRIVES OF EGO-SELF

There is nothing wrong with having needs. As human beings we are born with a few basic needs that must be satisfied. Human beings are part of the animal kingdom, and we share four basic, innate needs with all other members of the animal kingdom: self-preservation, food, sleep and sex. Every living thing finds some way to protect itself (self-preservation), some way to gain nourishment (food), some way to rest and rejuvenate (sleep), and some way to procreate (sex). These primitive needs are compelling drives since they insure the survival of both the individual and the species. They are built into the fabric of the body/mind complex and are fully operational when we are born.

The most powerful of these innate drives is self-preservation. We will do whatever is necessary to protect ourselves. This is not the same as fear. Fear is a learned emotional reaction. No human child is born with fear, but we are each born with a powerful urge for self-preservation. The difference between the two is great. Think of driving in your automobile and coming close to having a very bad accident. At that moment, you will have one of two experiences. The most typical experience is a strong fear reaction. Your body's automatic response to this fear is the fight-or-flight reaction. Your muscles become very tense, your heart and blood pressure increase dramatically, you feel your heart in your throat, you break out in a cold sweat, your stomach does flip-flops, your breathing either stops or becomes very fast and shallow and you can't think clearly.

We think that the fight-or-flight reaction protects us, and to some degree it does. But an extreme reaction can actually immobilize us and increase the chances of being harmed—like a deer caught in headlights. Intense fear places enormous stress on the body, and the hormonal changes that take place during this reaction may last as long as two or three weeks. The effects on the mind are just as terrible. In fact, we often become fearful simply by remembering this awful experience and create still another fight-or-flight reaction.

Fear is a very strong word, and most of us don't like to think of ourselves as fearful. Instead, we talk about our worries and concerns. But worry is just another name for fear, and these small fears create slight fight-or-flight reactions. These reactions may not be intense, but they are constant, resulting in chronic conditions of stress which lead to disease and close down the creative resources of the mind. To some extent, the fight-or-flight reaction does protect us, but the cost for this protection is always high and, in some cases, tragic.

On the other hand, when self-preservation dominates the mind, we will respond differently to the same event. You may recall experiencing a close call during which everything started happening in slow motion. If you remember this event clearly, you will recall that your heart did not race, your muscles were not tense, and you remained relaxed, calm and clear-minded. You knew exactly what action to take to protect yourself without thinking about it. You did not have a fight-or-flight reaction, and there was no stress in your body or fear in your mind.

A participant in a stress-management seminar recalled just such an incident. He was alone in his car, driving down the highway at seventy miles per hour, following a flatbed semi-trailer truck. On the truck were four pieces of steel. Suddenly, the restraints holding the steel broke, and one of the pieces flew off the truck, and headed straight for the man's windshield. At that moment, it seemed to him that time slowed to a crawl. The steel seemed to move at a snail's pace. Without thinking, he knew exactly how far he could move his car out of the lane without hitting oncoming traffic, and he had all the time he needed to take action to keep himself from being hit. The piece of steel went through the passenger side of the front window, passed through the front and the back seat, and embedded itself in the trunk of the car. He maintained his calmness and clarity of mind and was able to signal the truck in front of him to pull over.

The whole incident took no longer than a few quick seconds, yet for him, the event became timeless. He had no fear or stress. This dramatic change in his experience of time and space was created by the powerful drive for self-preservation. It provided him with everything he needed to protect himself without resorting to the costly fight-or-flight reaction.

No human being is born with fear. It is a learned emotional reaction, a habit of the mind and body that leads to stress, disease, danger and loneliness. Every human being is born with the powerful drive of self-preservation. But even this necessary drive can be twisted to serve the purposes of the ego—to protect the ego-self as well as the physical body. In fact, we will do things that are actually harmful or that threaten our physical body—smoking, drinking and driving, taking chances to show off, even go to war—in order to aggrandize the ego-self. For example, animals have a strong sense of self-preservation, but they don't go to war. But when humans' religious, economic or political beliefs are threatened, war is often the response.

It's easy to find threatened ego-selves, particularly when status is involved. "Road rage," angry, reckless driving that occurs when an impatient, frustrated motorist believes that another driver has intentionally slowed him or her down or cut him or her off, is a perfect example. Self-preservation is sublimated to the ego's need for supremacy, and the result is disaster.

In love relationships, this ego-self is often easily threatened. Our sense of self-worth and value is often determined by whether or not someone loves us more than anyone else. This is a recipe for disaster. The more insecure and dependent we become, the more desperately we try to maintain the relationship. This only increases the problems in the relationship, which then snowball into even greater emotional disturbances. O. J. Simpson's remarks clearly show how the ego-self can distort love and justify even violence to protect itself.

The other primitive drives, for food, sleep and sex, are also powerful. As long as we find ways to satisfy them, we don't really experience their power to motivate us. But when there is no food, people will walk for hundreds of miles to find something to eat. When we are tired, we will sleep, no matter how fearful or hungry we are. And we know just how influential the drive to procreate can be. Simply look at advertising in our culture. As any ad agency knows well, sex sells!

THE POWER OF DESIRE

When one of these four primitive needs is stimulated, we become energized. Our mind quickly directs that energy towards finding a solution. When the energy generated by one of the four primitive urges is directed toward a specific object, it is called desire. That object may be a thing, such as a new car, a new dress or a vacation home. It may also be a person, such as a lover or mate. It could also be a religious belief or a certain course of action. For example, when we are hungry, we begin very quickly to desire specific foods that would satisfy us.

Desire is the real motivation behind the actions of the ego-self. The stronger the desire, the more motivated we become. In the world of professional sports, it's well known that one of the key characteristics of a championship team is a strong desire to win. In fact, success in any aspect of life depends more on desire for success than on education, opportunity or even talent. If our desire for a particular goal is strong, nothing can prevent us from satisfying it.

This is not true for wants. We want many things, and we don't always get what we want. Truth be told, we want an uncountable number of things, but our real desires are few. I may want a new car, but I probably won't buy one until my financial condition improves. I may think about it occasionally, or even visit a car dealer. But as long as it remains simply something I would like to have, I will not move heaven and earth to buy it. If I don't get the car, I shrug it off and go on thinking about other things.

But if I really desire that car, if my mind sees that car as crucial to my personal happiness and well-being, I *will* move heaven and earth to buy it. Look, for instance, at just how crucial a role personal image plays in automobile advertising. If the advertising can stimulate the desire for ego-enhancement (self-preservation), I will find a way to buy that car, even if it is ultimately harmful to me to do so. If we truly desire something, we spend every moment, every thought and every effort to obtain it. Isn't this what love songs and poetry are all about?

Desire is a powerful force, and it demands expression and satisfaction. But, it is not intelligent. If we don't direct it with skill and discrimination, desires will create all sorts of problems for us. Our good judgment can be overwhelmed by its power, and we may end up doing things that we later regret. Understanding how to direct this powerful force is essential to our emotional health, well-being and success.

EMOTIONAL ATTACHMENT:
CONFUSING DESIRE WITH LOVE

What we typically call love is love clouded by desire. This so-called love stems from the pleasure and satisfaction we feel when our needs are satisfied; it is not an expression of the spiritual Self. The ego-self wants to secure whatever gives pleasure, security or contentment.

When we gain physical or emotional pleasure from being with some-one, or from some particular thing, then we say that we love that person or thing. The more pleasure we feel, the more we believe that our love is strong. On the other hand, if we experience pain, then we say we hate that person or thing. We become angry when a person doesn't return our love in the way we want. It doesn't really matter whether or not this individual wants to love us back or is even capa-ble of loving us in the way we want. We want what we want when we want it! Heaven help the poor individual who cannot live up to our expectations, particularly if we "love" him or her.

We confuse love with the desire for pleasure and then think hate is the opposite of love. Pleasure and pain both create strong emotional habits in the mind. We then become dependent on a person for pleasure (happiness), or we spend a great deal of effort trying to avoid the pain created by our dependency to that person. This dependency is called "emotional attachment."

Physical pleasure or pain are powerful influences, but emotional pleasure or pain are even stronger. Consequently, the ego-self tries to avoid pain and seek pleasure. It wants to own whatever makes it feel good and avoid whatever makes it feel bad. The weaker the ego-self, the more it wants to grasp any little pleasure or security. Consequently, the more self-centered it becomes, the more pain it creates for itself. In other words, the more we try to hold on, the less loving we become and the greater our loneliness.

Parents get caught in this cycle as easily as lovers do. The natural progress is for children to grow up and become independent individ-uals. But if parents live their lives through their children and depend on them to make them feel successful, for attention, or to make them feel needed or important, they inevitably suffer from the empty nest syndrome. These parents often resort to guilt and manipulation in order to maintain control over their children. They claim to love their children, but in fact, they really need their children to make them feel good (loved, secure, important) about themselves. A healthy ego-self will miss the children when they move out but will do everything possible to help them to grow strong, independent and free, capable of loving without guilt. The weaker the ego-self, the more the parent will hold on to the children, manipulate them with guilt and obligation and suffer from their absence.

By confusing love and desire, we create problems of emotional dependency. Desire almost always leads to dependency on the object of desire. Pure love cannot miss anyone because pure love doesn't need anyone. As an expression of the Divine, pure love is complete within itself. Love flows from the spiritual Self. When we are loving, we experience fulfillment and joy with no thought of *I, me* or *mine* at the time. We are, at least temporarily, free from the demands, fears and desires of the ego-self.

All human beings have emotional needs, and a strong, healthy ego finds successful ways to satisfy them. We enter relationships to satisfy our needs, and when this is done with genuine love, both partners benefit. But, when emotional dependency becomes the focus, instead of selfless love, we stop giving and demand something in return for attention and affection. In other words, we reinforce our ego-self and create loneliness. Even worse, this emotional attachment always leads to fear since the ego-self always fears to lose what is important to *itself.*

The cure for emotional attachment is to practice nonattachment, consciously giving up the need to have, or own, a particular outcome, person, place or thing. This does not mean that we are detached or passive about life, that we avoid relationships or deny our feelings. Nonattachment means that we recognize that the things of the world are there for us to use, but not to own. We do not allow ourselves to be emotionally dependent on the objects of our desires. Through experience with the spiritual Self we discover that we alone are the source of our happiness and unhappiness, satisfaction or dissatisfaction. The more skilled we become at non-attachment, the less troubled we are with emotional disturbances of all kinds. In chapter 5 we will explore this critical skill in depth.

There is nothing wrong with primitive drives. They si[...]
what they are. There is nothing inherently wrong, sinful or e[...]
the sex drive, just as there is nothing wrong with the drive for sleep,
food or self-preservation. We do not criticize animals for being animals. If a lion uses its superior power to kill a baby gazelle, we do not
put the lion on trial. We recognize that the lion is only acting according to its nature. All life is provided with the necessary means to
protect, sustain and procreate itself. Primitive drives should be recognized and honored as the integral expression of a wise, loving and
nurturing Mother Nature.

THE HUMAN DIFFERENCE

But we would certainly put a human being on trial for killing the off-
spring of his or her neighbor. We know that there is something
different in humans—a flexibility, an intelligence, a sense of free will,
an ability to choose—that uniquely characterizes the human animal.
This difference is the unique human capacity for "reflective awareness,"
the ability to be aware of our own thinking.

Reflective awareness is not the same thing as thinking. Thinking
is a mental process that allows the brain to collect and organize sensory data, analyze it, make discriminations, and eventually arrive at a
conclusion. It involves all the different aspects of the mind: memory,
belief, emotions and habits. Thinking is part of the ego-self, and, consequently, by thinking alone, we cannot go beyond the ego-self.
Whatever we *think* is only a pattern of the mind, not the actual reality of who we are. It is a very noisy, demanding activity that conceals
the spiritual Self.

Through reflective awareness, human beings can step back and
observe their urges, postpone fulfilling their desires, and travel the
world to find that perfect mate or a specifically desired food. In other
words, we are not absolutely controlled by our primitive drives. Reflective awareness provides us with the power to choose how we fulfill
these needs, and even whether we will satisfy them or not. Even

during a crisis, we can satisfy our needs. We can satisfy the ego-self's need for love, affection and affiliation without creating the anxiety of loneliness. Whether or not we use that capacity skillfully is another thing altogether.

The capacity to reflect on our thoughts and urges marks the most significant difference between humans and all other animals. Clearly, animals think. If you have ever tried to keep the squirrels out of your bird-feeder, you know just how smart animals can be. Animals also communicate, form societies, and some, like some humans, mate for life. But there is no evidence anywhere that animals are aware of their thoughts. It is this power of reflective awareness, the ability to witness or observe our own thinking, that separates the human being from the rest of the animal kingdom.

Animals are controlled by their nature—whatever primitive urge is strongest at the moment. For instance, when hungry, an animal will eat whatever is immediately available as long as it is an appropriate part of its food chain. Most people are terrified by snakes, yet there is very little reason for this fear. We are not part of a snake's food chain, and, as long as we don't threaten them, they have very little interest in us. A human being, on the other hand, will pass up healthful food and consume things that nature never intended—diet soft drinks, cigarettes, food additives. We don't have to mate with every male or female that offers an opportunity, but our ability to choose can immensely complicate this aspect of life. Human beings have the fortitude to resist the powerful urges of the primitive drives and to shape their expression. We do not have to be dominated by them. We have the freedom to choose how to satisfy primitive drives. To the degree that we are free from emotional attachment, we can exercise this freedom.

Law, philosophy and religion result from our capacity for reflection. Unfortunately, many of us do not utilize this capacity very skillfully. It doesn't take more than a glance at the morning paper to realize that much of what we do can hardly be called human. We often let the animal nature dominate our thoughts and behavior.

But reflective awareness provides us with the power to respond rather than react, the freedom to choose something different, to redirect our actions, to make choices. Reflective awareness allows us to quiet the noisy mind and to become aware of a deeper truth. This is the human difference—not that we can think, but that we can step away from the mind and its compulsions, habits and desires and see things from the higher perspective of our spiritual Self.

THE SPIRITUAL CONNECTION

We do not have to be slaves to desires and drives. We can experience the power and freedom of pure love. Love stems from a single source, the spiritual Self. Without hesitation, most of us refer to ourselves, and others, as consisting of body, mind *and* spirit. We are pretty comfortable talking about the body and mind, but when it comes to spirit, we can get pretty confused. This dimension of human reality is less familiar, even though we have all kinds of beliefs about it. Unfortunately, most of us only have our beliefs and very little direct experience of the spiritual Self. Consequently, we have little ability to use the powerful resources that characterize the spiritual Self. We don't experience its practical power in our day-to-day life. As a result, we remain stuck in the ego-self and suffer its limitations.

To be fully human means to bring together and coordinate body, mind and spirit. In a sense, a human being is the marriage of the eternal and the non-eternal, of spirit and matter, of consciousness and energy, of timelessness and time. The ego is a function of the mind and only knows body and mind. It likes to think that it alone is the center of the universe. A healthy, strong ego can expand to include others as part of itself. But it will still see itself as the owner of human experience.

But the ego is only a tool of the mind, and not its owner. The ego-self is not the center of the universe, but rather the general manager of the body/mind complex. Its sole purpose is to coordinate the various functions and operations of the personality so we can use the mind and body in a consistent, integrated and effective way to benefit the spiritual Self.

The true owner of our real identity is the spiritual Self. It is the only unchanging, eternal, nonmaterial Reality. It is not the center of the universe, but an expression of the Universal Divinity, a spark of the unchanging, eternal Truth that we call God. This core spiritual Self expresses its will through its tool, the material personality (the body/mind complex). This spiritual Self *is* the love that is expressed by the ego-self. Pure love is omniscient, omnipotent and eternal. The experience of this love is empowering, freeing and unforgettable. It puts an end to suffering, fear and loneliness.

The great yogic sages refer to this spiritual Self as *Satchitananda*—Existence, Consciousness and Bliss. It is pure Existence, eternal, without change; pure Consciousness, without any object; and pure Bliss, the fulfillment and expression of Love.

A PROBLEM OF IGNORANCE

The proper function of the ego is to create a limited sense of I-ness. The problem is that we identify with this limited sense of I-ness. We believe that this unique individuality is all that we are. We don't recognize that the mind and body are simply tools for us to use. The personality is not our real identity. It is a limited projection of our will. We suffer from loneliness (and all sorts of other miseries) because we accept the ego's limited definition of Self.

If we were to meet and I asked you who you are, what would be your answer? You would probably tell me your name and occupation. And as we spoke, you would reveal different aspects of your personality. If I were to meet you again, several years later, you would be a different person. Your body would have changed, your job might have changed, even your behavior, emotions and thoughts would have changed. If I were to ask the same question again, would you say that you are the same person or someone different? What is it that would not have changed? What core Self consistently projects itself through the personality? Who is it that is aware of the body and the changes the body goes through? Who is it that is aware of the thoughts and emotions and all their changes?

This is the heart of the issue. We are usually not conscious of the core identity, the spiritual Self that directs the entire personality through the force of will. Lacking this awareness, we identify with the thoughts and feelings, the courage and fears and the conflicts and resolutions which occur in the mind and make up the personality. This leaves us stuck within the limits of the ego, and we suffer from loneliness. This lack of awareness is called ignorance.

Ignorance doesn't refer to intelligence or to the number of educational degrees we earn. Many educated, intelligent people are woefully ignorant. Ignorance means *to ignore, to be unaware of, to be unconscious of.* We are unaware of our spiritual core, the unlimited, universal Self that is our true identity and our greatest friend. We are out of touch with pure love and its power to bring us to personal greatness.

We think we consist only of body and mind because our limited experience tells us so. But in truth, we are pure Consciousness, or Soul, if you will. If we do not experience this powerful spiritual Self and lack awareness of its reality, we have no choice but to identify with the ego-self. This ignorance is the root cause of loneliness. At one level, loneliness reflects the separateness we feel from other humans; at another level, it reflects the isolation we feel from ourselves; at yet another, it reflects the separateness we feel from nature. But at the heart of all loneliness is the separateness we experience from our spiritual Self, from God.

SELFLESSNESS: THE PURE FLAME OF LOVE

The separation from the spiritual Self is a separation from the experience of pure love. Isolated from this essential love, we go to great lengths trying to find it outside of ourselves. Chasing illusion after illusion, we end up disillusioned with ourselves, with others and with life. This is all part of the primal ignorance, believing that we are only the mind/body complex of the ego-self. The only cure is to put an end to ignorance and become conscious of the spiritual Self.

Fortunately, the task is simple: to rediscover the love that we already are. Although simple, it is by no means an easy task. The ingrained patterns of mind and body are aligned against us in this quest. We are trained to think about external realities but poorly equipped to focus on the inner realities. Our culture has shaped us to be "action freaks," ready to get busy, to change things and to take charge. This motivation is entirely within the realm of the ego-self. In and of itself, this is not a bad thing. But if this is all we know, we never understand the spiritual Self.

This journey to the spiritual Self is not one of learning and action, but of unlearning and acceptance. It does not involve grasping new ideas and beliefs, but rather, letting go of the compulsion of desires and fears. Observation and being are the focus, not making immediate and abrupt changes. We must let go of thoughts, desires and fears, not create new ones. Belief is not necessary, but an abiding curiosity and the willingness to experiment are essential. The truth is already inside of us; we need only rediscover that something which is already there.

The goal of the journey is the mystical experience, the conscious awareness of the spiritual Self. This experience is called by many names. In tantra, it is called *sabija samadhi,* consciousness without an object. In Christianity, it is called the "mystical experience;" in Taoism, the "Living Tao;" in Zen Buddhism, *satori.* The experience of the spiritual Self is the only real cure of loneliness, fear and self-hatred.

CHAPTER 4

JOURNEY INTO WHOLENESS

The most ancient traveler in the world is love,
which travels from eternity to eternity.

A great and holy man had lived his life dedicated to the will of God.
He became so filled with grace that any prayer he uttered was imme-
diately fulfilled. His heart was generous and kind, and he was a great
inspiration to all who knew him. As he grew in the Spirit, his knowl-
edge and wisdom became legendary. And when he died, many grieved
at the loss of such a great person. At the time of his passing, he entered
the Gates of Heaven and knocked at the door of God's house.

"Who is there?" demanded God.

"It is I, thy faithful servant," responded the holy man.

"Oh yes, my beloved child, I am overjoyed to see you," replied God.
"You have done very well, and I am pleased with you. But there is still
some work to be done. Please return for another life and continue your
good work."

The great man was reborn and again spent an exemplary life,
becoming even wiser and more enlightened than before. Through prayer
and meditation, he gained such clarity of mind that he could explain
the most profound scriptures in such simple terms and with such clar-
ity that even the simplest would gain insight. His love for God and
others was so immense that his name became synonymous with the word
"love." All who came into his presence experienced a profound change of
heart. Enemies would become friends, criminals would turn to chari-
table works, and those in distress would find peace and harmony.
Finally, the great sage again passed from the physical plane. Approach-
ing the house of God, he knocked at the door.

"Who is there?" asked God.

"It is I, thy faithful servant," cried the great sage.

"Oh yes, my beloved son. I am pleased with you and overjoyed to see you," said God. "But still, there is some work you must do. Please, return for another life and continue your wonderful work."

Again, the sage returned to be reborn. In this lifetime, the sage, along with prayer and meditation, began to ponder the great truths of his insights and experiences. He began to realize that everywhere he looked, everything he saw, was only another manifestation of the Divine Will. He saw God in the murderer as well as the saint, in the storm as well as in the sunset, in every creature and every rock. Contradictions and dualities resolved themselves in the power of his discrimination, imperfections dissolved in the power of his vision, and conflicts disappeared in the power of his love. With absolute clarity, he saw there was only one Reality, that only God existed. What he had previously seen as good and bad, as desirable and undesirable, as holy and unholy, was all nothing more than another manifestation of the Divine Will. Some who knew him hated him, some loved him. He saw all equally with a calm, clear and undisturbed mind and vision. When he passed from this life, only a fortunate few disciples knew what loss had taken place.

At this passing, when he arrived at God's home, again he knocked at the door.

"Who is there?" demanded God.

"Thine Own Self," replied the sage.

"Enter and be welcome, my beloved," replied God.

IN OUR JOURNEY, we will use the pathways found in all great spiritual traditions: prayer, meditation and contemplation. Our first task will be to escape the trap of the ego-self. We do this through prayer, the path of the Heart, through which we learn to surrender to the Divine Will. This will free us from identifying with the ego-self, letting us tap into the power of our spiritual Self. Meditation is the path of the mind. Through meditation, we strengthen determination and develop full awareness of the spiritual Self through concentration and the expansion of consciousness. As we meditate, we become aware of inner wisdom and strength, enabling us to face life fearlessly and joyfully. Contemplation is the path of the intellect. Through contemplation, we refine inner wisdom to its final perfection and discriminate between the world of ego and the Reality of the spiritual Self.

PRAYER: THE POWER OF LOVE

We pray for many things—for victory in battle, for salvation, for material wealth and power, for the health and well-being of ourselves and others, even for wisdom, strength and enlightenment. But do we really understand what we do when we pray? Prayers are actions, and every action has its consequence. The stronger, more intense the action, the greater the consequence. Prayer is a focusing of our attention, and what we pay attention to, we reinforce and strengthen in our mind and life. The power of prayer stems from our ability to focus our emotional energy. Intensity requires concentration, and concentration requires commitment. Prayer is an act of total commitment, a channeling of all emotional energy into a specific outcome. When we aren't committed, prayer is empty and impotent and bears no fruit.

Prayer is the path of the heart. It is the most honest, simple and straightforward communication possible. It is an act of surrender, but not to another ego, a belief system or a material force. This we should never do. Nor is it an escape from personal responsibility for what we do or think. We can never escape responsibility for our actions, regardless of who or what we may blame.

True surrender acknowledges the power of love. Prayer is first and foremost a recognition and awareness of a reality greater than the individual personality—the overwhelming love that characterizes the mystical Self, that spark of God that resides within every human being. Prayer creates personal transformation and opens our own hearts to the Grace and Power of the Divine.

We don't always experience this Grace because our prayers are often nothing more than wish lists, clouded by the wants, desires and fears of the ego-self. There are basically two kinds of prayers—God-centered prayer and ego-centered prayer. In our modern culture, prayer often expresses the desire for achievement—success, prosperity, wealth and health. This is, pure and simple, ego-centered prayer. We use ego-centered prayer to beg for material things from God, to negotiate our way out of difficult and painful situations and even to wreak havoc, death, and destruction on our enemies, including their families, homes and nation.

EGO-CENTERED PRAYER:
REINFORCING LONELINESS

Most of our prayers do not search the depths of the heart, or consider the consequences if our wishes were to come true. The ego-self is in command, and we think only of what fits our own narrow, selfish needs. This doesn't make us bad people, only ego-centered people, alienated from the spiritual Self. The inevitable outcome is profound loneliness.

The great American author Mark Twain (Samuel Clemens) wrote about ego-centered prayer in *The War Prayer*, a story that he wouldn't allow to be published until after his death. He believed that only dead men knew the truth, and that this work was to be a revelation of truth. It tells a story about people attending Sunday service at a local church. This service is dedicated to offering prayers and good wishes for the young men of the town who are going off to war. In the middle of a long and fervent prayer calling for victory for the young soldiers and utter defeat for the enemy, the doors of the church suddenly and noisily burst open. An old man, with a long, flowing beard and dressed in strange clothing, walks boldly down the aisle and up to the lectern. Brushing the startled minister aside, the old man turns to the audience and states that he has been sent by Almighty God to reveal to them exactly what they are praying for.

Then he makes clear the awful consequences should the prayers of the congregation be granted. Utter defeat for the enemy would mean the destruction of families and homes, the killing and maiming of innocent children, the destruction of food supplies and the terrible consequences of great hunger and disease. When he finishes, silence fills the church, and the old man asks if that is what the church members really want God to grant. Then the old man walks out of the church and disappears. It is later agreed that the old man is mentally deranged, and he is soon forgotten.

This was not one of Mark Twain's most popular works. In fact, most people have never heard of it. I suspect this is because he was right—it contains the truth. We do pray for harm to fall on others when we pray for advantage over them. We don't want to face this shameless egotism because, at the spiritual level, we know the suffering that would come to others if these prayers were answered.

The individual human mind is a powerful tool. When we focus on something with intensity and persistence, we can bring it to pass. Ego-centered prayer does bear fruit, particularly when offered with focus and emotional intensity. But this fruit only strengthens the ego-self, which leads to even greater isolation and loneliness.

GOD-CENTERED PRAYER:
BREAKING THE CHAINS OF EGO

In pure God-centered prayer, we acknowledge our connection to God. Pure prayer is selfless in its supplication. When we are engaged in God-centered prayer, the I-ness no longer exists. Individuality and all the things that go with it—assertiveness, wishing and demanding, begging for this and that—disappear in surrender to Divine Will. In pure prayer, we seek only wisdom and strength. It is desireless. There is no wishing for a particular outcome or material gain, no self-congratulatory thanks for victory, only the humble acceptance of Grace.

And yet it is the most fulfilling of all prayers because it fills us with the presence of the Divine Will. Pure prayer is powerful, transformative and freeing. In the moment of God-centered prayer, we are no longer bound by the fears, desires, limits and conditions of the ego-self. Filled with the awareness of the spiritual Self, we break free of ego-centered concerns. Fears, self-hatred and loneliness disappear as we are filled with the Grace of Divine Will.

Through God-centered prayer, we open the heart chakra, the seat of the soul, and we experience the pure, egoless love that characterizes the spiritual Self. This transformation breaks the terrible chains of the ego-self, and we fully experience our identity as the spiritual Self. This simple act of God-centered prayer is more powerful than all the knowledge we may gather. It transforms fears, hatred, anger and self-ishness into compassion, tranquillity and love.

But this simple act is not easy to achieve. Along with emotional commitment, God-centered prayer requires at least two other quali-ties: complete humility and absolute honesty. True humility does not mean being a doormat or being passive and weak. It is, in fact, just the opposite. Through humility, we express our inner strength as we join forces with the power of our mystical Self. Genuine humility is the conscious recognition that we are part of something much greater than ourselves. It is the feeling that takes hold when we witness the birth of a child or when we spend time looking up at the stars on a clear, dark night. It fills the heart with wonder, respect and gratitude without diminishing us in any way. During these times, we never expe-rience solitude as loneliness, nor do we feel isolated and alone. Humility frees us from the powerful grasp of the ego, and when we are free from the ego, we are free from loneliness.

It seems odd that we are sometimes dishonest when we pray. Everything is already known to the Divine. Absolutely nothing about the personality can be hidden or denied to God. But when we fail to be absolutely honest in our effort, we cheat ourselves. We hide from our own perceived weaknesses and thereby strengthen the ego. The Christian tradition offers the phrase "The truth shall set you free." In prayer, when we honestly face the ego-self and the patterns, twists and turns of the personality and surrender them to the Divine, we free ourselves from the grasp of the ego. At that moment of truth, we are filled with the Light of the spiritual Self and experience the Grace of God.

It isn't the words we use that make a prayer a prayer, but rather the purity of our intent. An old story from the Russian Orthodox tradition illustrates the power of pure prayer. On the death of the old metropolitan, a new religious leader was chosen. The new metropolitan was kind and conscientious, having a great desire to serve the priests and monks under his charge. He traveled far and wide, visiting the different churches and monasteries and offering whatever help was needed. He came to know of a small monastery located on a tiny island on Lake Baikal. To his dismay, the records revealed that no metropolitan had visited this small monastery for nearly thirty years. Apparently, there were only three monks there, and, according to the records, they had been left alone for all this time.

Wishing to correct this oversight, the metropolitan immediately hired a large boat and set sail for the island. The three monks, now rather elderly, were overjoyed to be visited by their spiritual leader and made every effort to make him comfortable. The metropolitan, concerned about their spiritual growth, asked the monks about their prayers.

"We have never been taught any prayers," said one of the monks. "So we simply pray, 'Thou art three and we are three. Bless us, O Lord.'"

Smiling to himself at their naïveté, the metropolitan kindly said, "Oh my, I can see that no one has taught you to pray the official prayers of the church. Come, my friends, and I will teach you how to say the prayers."

The monks were overjoyed by this kindness and generosity. For several hours they listened to the official prayers taught by the metropolitan. Finally, it was time for him to return to the far-off mainland.

The monks were grateful to the metropolitan for giving so

generously of his time and knowledge. "Thank you, Holy Father," they said. "Your kind attention and instruction will be reverently received and practiced. Please pray for us that we may follow the correct path."

The metropolitan gave his final blessings and sailed off. The spiritual leader was pleased with himself that he had taken the time and trouble to visit these poor, elderly monks and to teach them the proper way to pray.

Several hours into his journey, the skies darkened, and a great storm came upon the ship. The waves grew in size, and the ship was tossed here and there. Suddenly, as the metropolitan watched the storm clouds, he was stunned by an amazing sight. Illuminated by great lightning flashes, the three elderly monks were running as fast as they could above the surface of the waves toward the ship.

"Holy Father," they cried as they came closer to the ship. "Please forgive us; we have forgotten the prayers you have so generously taught us. We want so much to pray to God in the right way. Please, be kind enough to repeat them for us once more."

The metropolitan sank to his knees. "Forgive me," he said to the monks. "Please forget all that I so arrogantly taught you. Pray as you have always done, and be kind enough to pray for me, that I might learn to pray as you three do."

It is the heart that counts in prayer, not the "correct" words or the form. All spiritual traditions are filled with stories and parables about how the naive prayers of innocent children and uneducated people achieve Divine Grace, whereas the prayers of the learned and anointed do little. When we empty our mind and open our hearts, whatever prayer we think, feel or say becomes an opening for Divine Grace. In this acknowledgment of our connection to the Divine, we feel the inner force of the mystical Self that we call love. Prayer is accessible to anyone. Past actions, belief systems, culture—none matter if one faces the Divinity with humility, honesty and surrender. Like sunshine and life-giving rain, there is no discrimination in Divine Grace if the heart is pure.

THE PRACTICE OF PRAYER

To pray is simple, it is a matter of attention and surrender. All religious traditions have prayers. Depending on your particular belief, you may stand, sit, even lie prone to pray. The different postures attempt to demonstrate humility and enhance feelings of surrender. It really doesn't matter what position the body is in, the critical factor is what happens inside the mind and heart. The best way to prepare for prayer is simply to relax and focus on what is most important to you. Speak of your concerns in an honest and straightforward way. Don't get fancy. Big words may impress the ego, but they don't impress God. Speak simply and from your heart, with feeling. Surrender occurs when you genuinely trust that the Divine will bear the burden of your concerns, and that God will always protect and guide you, as well as all others.

Prayer quiets the heart as we speak our innermost thoughts to the Divine. It is always a personal communication, even when done with others. We may pray for the benefit of others, for the relief of suffering, and especially for wisdom and strength to face the tasks that life presents. It is the act of surrender to Divine Will—"not my will, but Thy will be done"—that characterizes God-centered prayer. At the end of prayer, there should be a period of silence. Clear the mind of all thoughts using breath awareness, and simply listen and relax. Allow yourself time to feel the Divine's response of confirming Grace.

For example, most of us worry needlessly about our children's safety. Of course, we take what necessary steps we can, but we realize that we cannot always be with them to protect them. When you worry about your children, sit quietly and give voice to your concerns. Speak quietly as if someone was actually sitting next to you, listening to your words. Vocalizing your concerns provides an opportunity to clarify your thoughts and feelings. After speaking what is in your heart, surrender your children's well-being to the Divine. After all, if God does not protect your children, how could you possibly do so? If you sincerely surrender their care, you will experience a sense of quiet release and relief as you realize that the Divine is in charge of your children's lives just as It is yours.

Pray for what is meaningful to you—your personal thoughts and feelings or the prayers of your own tradition. Do not beg for material things, but pray for wisdom, strength and guidance. Make the Divine the center of your prayer and not the desires, wants and fear of the ego, and you will realize that God has already granted your prayers. In a moment, loneliness will disappear, and you will be free from the fears, self-hatred and limitations of the ego-self. It is no wonder that we call this Amazing Grace.

MEDITATION: THE PATH OF THE MIND

Through God-centered prayer, we lose our attachment to the ego-self and surrender to Divine Will. But there is another step. In the moment of surrender created through prayer, we feel the power of God, but we experience that power as a Reality outside of ourselves. Even though refined and purified by Divine Grace, the ego-self still exerts its hold on our identity. We still feel and see ourselves as separate from God. As long as we experience God as separate from ourselves, as some external Reality, we will suffer the pangs of loneliness. Through God-centered prayer, we loosen the hold of the ego-self, but we still remain caught in its limitations. Instead of loneliness for others, we now experience loneliness for God. The great saints and sages referred to this experience when they spoke of the terrible longing for God.

Whereas prayer is the path of the heart, meditation is the path of the mind. Actually, it is a journey *through* the mind. As long as we remain identified with the mind, we are limited by its functions, including the ego. But as we refine the power of meditation, we penetrate this veil called mind and experience the super-conscious state of the spiritual Self. Through meditation, we expand the limited conscious awareness that we use in our daily life and expand it into total Consciousness, the full awareness of the spiritual Self, the spark of God that is our real identity. The spiritual Self, the very core of our being, is no longer an intellectual concept, a belief or even a hope or faith. It becomes our direct experience. Through meditation, we gradually transform our sense of identity from the ego-self to the spiritual Self.

I can vividly recall my first two experiences of realizing that I wasn't my body or mind. The first happened when my spiritual master led me through a concentration exercise called "61 Points." In this exercise, you focus on sixty-one different points in the body, visualizing a small blue star, or flame, at each point. These points correspond to various energy centers in the body. When we had completed the exercise, he instructed me to focus on a white light in the heart center in the middle of my chest. Suddenly, I was no longer a physical body lying on the carpet, I had become the light itself. In a moment I became free of the limits of body consciousness and realized that I could be anywhere in the universe that I chose to be. I felt a great tranquillity and peace. This lasted for several minutes, ending only when I suddenly focused on my breathing.

The second occurrence happened several months later and was even stronger. I had been practicing meditation for about fifteen minutes when, suddenly, a piercing white light appeared in my awareness. Again, I became this light, and I realized, without a shadow of any doubt, that everything—the house I was sitting in, my body, my family and friends, my job, my entire world—could be destroyed, but that *I* would continue on. I cannot say for how long that moment existed, but, in that moment, my entire world shifted as I experienced my own eternal nature. Half of the fears and worries that bedeviled me disappeared from my mind and never returned. In that one experience, my life shifted direction.

Most people, even many who claim to teach meditation, don't understand its nature or purpose. Some confuse meditation with imagery exercises, letting their imaginations create all sorts of fascinating scenes and opportunities. Others think it is a trance state, a trip into another world. Still others believe it to be a form of hypnosis, relaxation or contemplation. In the West, people typically meditate as a way to relieve stress, to increase self-confidence, achieve greater clarity of thought and open the creative force of the mind. Real meditation will do all of this and more. It is the most effective tool available for strengthening the mind.

Meditation is not a philosophy, a ritual, a trance or even a relaxation technique. *Meditation is a refined state of effortless, unbroken concentration on a single point over an extended period of time.* It is not thinking, but perception; a process of observation that leads to increased awareness. Meditation is not a noun, but a verb. It is not an end product, but a process that leads to silence, and from silence to *samadhi*, the direct, conscious awareness of the spiritual Self. In Western terms, this is called the "mystical experience." Meditation is a spiritual exercise that leads to complete conscious awareness of the spiritual Self as the true substance of the personality.

The analogy of light helps explain the connection between concentration and awareness. When we walk into a lighted room, we are able to see what is in the room because of light. Light actually consists of individual units of energy called photons. These photons bounce off objects and illuminate them. Although we don't feel the light, it illuminates whatever it strikes, and we become aware of what the light illuminates. If you are in a cave and the lights are extinguished, you experience total darkness. You can hold your hand as close as possible to your eyes, and you still will not see your hand. Without light, you lack the ability to see.

When the light strikes our skin, we don't feel photons because they are relatively weak and scattered by the time they reach us. But if we hold our hand next to the light, the photons will be strong and concentrated enough to create heat or even burn us. If we force these photons to go in the same direction at the same time, if we synchronize and concentrate these photons, we create a laser. Depending on how the laser is built, the light may be powerful enough to penetrate a steel plate or focused so precisely that it can be used for eye or brain surgery.

The energy of our mind behaves in the same way. Let's imagine that the individual units of mental energy are called "mentons." Typically, the mind reacts in a scattershot way to a constant stream of stimuli from both the outside world and our own thoughts, fears, desires, wants and needs. This weakens the mind and we have trouble thinking clearly and understanding anything. But by focusing our attention, we can organize and synchronize the energy of the mind. The more concentrated our attention, the more powerful the mind becomes and the more capable we will be of understanding the object of our attention. The more refined our power of concentration, the more laser-like we make our mind.

Psychologists talk about peak experiences, or going with the flow, experiences that happen only when we are highly focused on what we are doing. During these moments, we change our experience of time and space, understand things more completely, generate insight and knowledge, are most creative and do our best work. In this condition of intense concentration, the mind accesses an unusual depth of knowledge and creates understanding, and we feel a great deal of joy and satisfaction.

When such refined concentration has an inner focus, it is meditation. Meditation becomes a laser that penetrates the cloudy veil of the mind. Again, the analogy to light helps us to understand the power of meditation. Think of our normal conscious awareness as a beam of light. With our attention, we direct that light to illuminate, to make us more aware of (more conscious of) whatever we wish to understand. The more powerful our attention, the greater our concentration. This, in turn, increases the power of our beam of light and, consequently, increases our awareness, or consciousness.

The spiritual Self is like a great and perfect diamond that lies at the very end of a vast cave, which represents our mind. Our normal conscious awareness is like shining a small flashlight into the opening of a cave. Our attention is often weak and scattered, and so the light we bring to the cave of our mind is weak and scattered. Our awareness doesn't penetrate very far into the cave before it dissipates, leaving us unable to see the pathway through the cave. We easily become distracted and lost in the habits, desires and fears hidden in the unconscious mind. Consequently, most of us remain stuck within the limits of the ego-self, unaware of the powerful spiritual Self.

But if we use a laser instead of a flashlight, we can penetrate the depth of the cave and illuminate the pathway. If we synchronize the energy of the mind and create a laser mind, this concentration carries our awareness deep into the cave of the mind. We can now penetrate the darkness and the crevices of our mind and, we pass safely through and reach our diamond. As we expand our inner concentration, we gain greater awareness of our own wisdom and inner strength. At the culmination of our journey, we achieve *samadhi*, the tantric term for the mystical experience, and we become aware of the spiritual Self.

MEDITATION: THE INNER SCIENCE

The great meditative traditions are sophisticated internal, spiritual sciences, which are systematic, objective, experimental and verifiable. Rather than use the mind to research and study some external event, the object of study is the mind itself. The focus is on the internal reality. The foundation for knowledge is direct experience rather than analytic reasoning. This demands a rigorous introspection of uncompromising objectivity and honesty. Reasoning is utilized, but as a function of the mind, the reasoning process itself becomes part of the focus of study.

To be a great scientist requires enormous dedication and commitment to truth, wherever it leads. This same commitment and dedication are required of those who wish to realize the inner Truth. As an experiential science, the meditative traditions do not require belief. Rather, success in this science requires an overwhelming curiosity, a healthy skepticism paired with an open mind, and a willingness and the courage to experiment with oneself. To acquire spiritual knowledge requires much more than sitting twice a day and focusing on the word *one*. To achieve complete awareness of the spiritual Self entails deep commitment, the acquisition of knowledge based on direct experience and the necessary tools and techniques to do so. In other words, it takes both knowledge and skill to acquire Self-realization.

The only authentic guides are those who have actually made the journey and know the dynamics of inner development. Genuine masters are not masters of others, but masters of themselves. They have no interest in controlling others, only a great compassion to show others the pathways. They do not bestow enlightenment on their disciples. They understand that each individual must make that journey. They provide the knowledge and effective methodology, and they use their compassion and knowledge to help their disciples become strong, independent and free. Certification by organizations, by universities, or by yoga teacher associations are utterly useless in establishing authenticity of spiritual knowledge. Western preoccupation with degrees and certificates, over knowledge and experience, reflects ignorance and insecurity. Nor is popularity a good measure of spiritual knowledge or authenticity.

Finding qualified teachers is not difficult. It simply takes a little research and attention. There are well-known qualities to examine: background experience, capabilities and commitment, knowledge of the subject, dedication to teaching and personal qualities. But finding a genuine spiritual teacher is more difficult. Like precious jewels, genuine masters are rare and difficult to find. They do not seek out publicity, nor do they advertise for students. But here again, there are specific qualities to look for. The first and most important quality is selflessness. A spiritual master loves his disciples with a purity that transcends any self-centeredness. For twenty-five years I lived and studied with my spiritual master. During this time I never saw a single incidence of selfishness. He was completely dedicated to his disciples and his students' personal development. His love had the purity of a perfect diamond, and it was just as hard as a diamond. He was without mercy in his dedication to my personal development. Yet, even at the most difficult of times, it was very clear that whatever was happening was for the benefit of my spiritual development, not the satisfaction of some ego need of my master.

A genuine spiritual master seeks always to lead his or her disciples to independence and freedom. They are not herding or flocking creatures, striving to form associations, build large groups of followers or please public opinion. They fearlessly tread their path without concern for others' opinions. When deciding to follow a particular spiritual teacher, examine closely the fruits of the teaching. Look for the qualities of independence, strength and gentleness in the students of that teacher. Are they the kind of people you wish to become? Remember, a real master never asks for slavish acquiescence to the teaching, but cultivates an independent curiosity, a willingness to experiment and the strength to make your own decisions. The goal of all genuine spiritual masters is to lead you to the inner spiritual Self, not to become your personal savior.

Fortunately, the reality of the spiritual Self is available for anyone who will make the effort and begin to use this powerful tool called meditation. Those who earnestly seek spiritual knowledge will always find what they need. The quest should not be for a spiritual master, but for spiritual knowledge. Don't worry about finding a master, instead focus on learning and pursue your interests with as much commitment as you can muster. All traditions recognize that when the student is ready, the teacher will appear. The most important thing is to take the first step and begin to train the mind.

BEGINNING A MEDITATION PRACTICE

There are three inner focus points for refining concentration and developing a meditation practice: thoughts, images and sensations. The simplest focus point is the sensation of the breath. All meditation traditions focus first on breathing techniques to reduce stress, balance the body and mind and help bring conscious awareness into a useful focus. As the individual becomes more skilled, the focus point may change, depending upon the tradition. In the tantric tradition, breathing techniques become extremely sophisticated but give way to even more sophisticated inner concentration techniques involving both thoughts and images.

When a specific thought is used as a focus point, it is referred to as a "mantra." A mantra (thought form) is a movement of energy within the mind and is experienced as an inner sound. Mantra science is based on a profound, intricate knowledge of mind and energy, established through four thousand years of intense research and experience. Every thought we think has some impact on the mind, but that does not make it a mantra. Mantras are chosen because of their particular effect on the mind through concentration. Those who make up their own mantras or say that you can concentrate on any thought or sound, such as the word "one," are speaking out of profound ignorance of mantra science.

When a specific image is used as a focus point, it is referred to as a "yantra." Yantras are almost always mathematical symbols, such as an upward-pointing triangle with a dot in the middle of it surrounded by a circle. Like mantras, these highly refined images are chosen because they have a very definite and particular effect on the mind. Only those who have been trained in the science of mantra and yantra can teach others how to use these powerful tools effectively.

These inner focus points are typically focused on a specific area of the physical body which corresponds to one of the major centers of consciousness. These centers are called "chakras." There are seven major centers and many important minor ones. But for our purposes, we will speak of only two: the heart center, or *anahata chakra*, located along the spinal cord but represented as the area between the two breasts; and the mind or pineal center or *ajna chakra*, located directly above the brain stem and represented as the area between the two eye-brows (the so-called "third eye"). These two centers are primary focus points for meditation.

Very generally speaking, focusing on the pineal center works best for those who prefer to function on the basis of reasoning and logic, whereas focusing on the heart center is easier for those who prefer to function on the basis of emotion and feeling. One is not better than the other, but typically you will find one easier to concentrate on than the other. When beginning, use the one that seems easiest.

Mention of these spiritual centers is made in all great spiritual traditions, including Christianity. The Book of Revelation speaks of the seven seals as well as the seven cities. They represent these powerful centers of consciousness. These centers are deep spiritual realities, not superficial energy centers that can be manipulated like so many energy spigots. Chakras never go out of balance, they cannot be found in the body, and they are not brain, glandular or neurological centers. They are not the energy body, nor are they limited to the energy channels that sustain the connection between mind and body. They are not easily accessible to introspection. To gain knowledge of the chakras, we must be skilled enough in meditation to go beyond the mind. As spiritual energy devolves into the subtle energies of the mind, it does so through chakras. These spiritual realities are hidden to all but the most skilled of travelers.

Anyone can easily learn to meditate, regardless of religious tradition. The following exercises provide an excellent starting point. The first step is to establish diaphragmatic breathing as your moment-to-moment breathing habit (shown in chapter 2). Once we have established a balanced autonomic system through proper breathing, we can begin to train the mind. Often, the easiest way to begin is by focusing on breathing. One very useful tool is breath awareness (also discussed in chapter 2). It provides a focus point and helps calm the mind and emotions, allowing you to concentrate more easily. Breath awareness is one of the most powerful tools for controlling moment-to-moment emotional reactions by giving you control over the mind chatter. Directions for using breath awareness as a meditation practice is given below.

BREATH AWARENESS MEDITATION

Close your eyes and sit in an erect posture. Relax the body, and for the first few moments, focus your attention on the feeling of the breath as it enters and leaves the nostrils. There will be a slight touch of coolness on the inhalation and a very subtle touch of warmth on the exhalation. Don't think about the breath. Focus on the feeling of the breath. Then, by paying attention to the feeling of the breath going in and out of the nostrils, determine the dominant (or open) nostril. This is the one through which the air flows most easily. Don't use your fingers; use only your sensitivity to determine which nostril is dominant. After determining the dominant nostril, focus your attention on it for several breaths.

Now switch your attention to the passive (or closed) nostril, the one where the air flow is blocked or diminished. Concentrate on this nostril, as you begin to feel the air moving freely through it, until it becomes the dominant nostril. After the air flows freely through this nostril for several breaths, bring your attention back to the first nostril, the one originally open. When you begin to feel the air flow freely through this first nostril, shift your attention to the center between both nostrils. Concentrate on the air flowing freely through both. (Air flowing freely through both nostrils indicates complete balance in the autonomic nervous system and between the hemispheres of the brain. During this experience, your concentration can deepen and intensify.)

Whenever your mind wanders to thoughts or other distractions, bring your attention back to the feeling of the breath. Sit very still, maintaining this focus for as long as you comfortably can. When you are ready to finish, gently wriggle your toes and fingers, and slowly raise your hands to your face. Holding the hands next to each other, palms facing you, open your eyes to the palms of your hands.

One of the most accessible focus points in the mind is the image of a candle flame or a light. Light is a key focus point in all meditative traditions. As meditation skills become more refined, a number of different yantras and images that utilize light can be effective as central focus points. In the pineal or mind center, envision the light of a candle flame. In the heart center, envision a soft, undefined white light. Again, it doesn't matter which one you choose; use the one that seems easiest to focus on. The specific instructions for using light as a focus point are given below.

FLAME MEDITATION—AJNA (MIND) CHAKRA

Begin this exercise seated in an erect posture with your eyes closed. For the first few moments, mentally scan the body, relaxing any tension you may find. Then, for a few minutes, practice breath awareness until you feel both nostrils open.

After a few moments of concentrating on both nostrils flowing freely, follow the next inhalation up as if you are following it into the center of your mind. It's as if you are turning your eyes inward and looking toward the very center of your brain. Then picture yourself sitting in the middle of the mind, watching the body breathe around you. At this point, experience the body like a shell around you. After a few more moments, be aware of where thoughts first arise in the mind. Very close to this point

is the center of the mind, a point of stillness and quiet-
ness. When you find this center, your body will become
effortlessly still and the mind very calm. You will notice
that thoughts, images and sensations seem to revolve
around this center, but within the center itself, it is very
quiet and peaceful. Enjoy this calm center for a few
moments.

This mind or pineal center is called the *ajna chakra*.
In this center, visualize a small, crystal candle flame.
Allow the flame to be as small, as perfect and as still as
your mind will allow it to be. Don't struggle with your
mind; focus on whatever kind of flame the mind presents.
Hold your attention on this flame for as long as you comfortably can. When your mind wanders, simply bring it
back or to the flame. The flame may move around, change
color, become more or less distinct. Let the flame change
in whatever way it does, simply maintain your focus on
it. The concentration should be focused in the center of
the body, not on the surface. Don't struggle or fight with
your mind. Let thoughts and feelings come and go.
Whenever you realize that you are not focusing on the
light, simply bring your attention back to it.

Sit very still, maintaining this focus for as long as you
comfortably can. When you are ready to finish, direct
your attention to the flow of breath through the inner
space of your body. Follow the next exhalation back up
and out the nostrils, and focus your attention on the feeling of the breath for a few moments. Then gently wriggle
your toes and fingers, and slowly raise your hands to
your face. Holding the hands next to each other, palms
facing you, open your eyes to the palms of your hands.
Maintain the inner calm and stillness you feel for as long
as possible throughout the day.

LIGHT MEDITATION—ANAHATA (HEART) CHAKRA

As above, begin your meditation with breath awareness. After a few moments, follow the next inhalation down into the lungs and focus on the heart center in the area of the chest between the two breasts. At this point visualize a small, white light in the very center of the chest. This light is not a flame, but a soft, white, undefined light like that of a bright, white streetlight that you are looking at from some distance away. Allow this light to expand until it fills the entire chest cavity and it seems as if you are sitting in the middle of the light, enjoying the silence. Again, whenever your mind wanders, bring it back to the light in your heart center. The concentration should be focused in the center of the body, not on the surface. Don't struggle or fight with your mind. Let thoughts and feelings come and go. Whenever you realize that you are not focusing on the light, simply bring your attention back to it.

Sit very still, maintaining this focus for as long as you comfortably can. When you are ready to finish, direct your attention to the flow of breath through the inner space of your body. Follow the next exhalation back up and out the nostrils, and focus your attention on the feeling of the breath for a few moments. Then gently wriggle your toes and fingers, and slowly raise your hands to your face. Holding the hands next to each other, palms facing you, open your eyes to the palms of your hands. Maintain the inner calm and stillness you feel for as long as possible throughout the day.

The most powerful tool for training the mind is mantra, the use of specific sounds (thought forms) in the mind. They are referred to as sound instead of thought because the practice is to listen to the sound of the mantra as the mind repeats it over and over again. So, instead of thinking about the mantra, you are actually listening to the mind think it for you. This reflects the reality that meditation is a perceptual event, not a thinking or analytic event. The key is to listen as closely as you can, almost as if you are trying to determine just exactly where in the mind you first perceive the mantra. It's almost as if you are trying to determine which brain cells are creating that sound form for you.

As you become more skilled with meditation, the sound gradually becomes a vibration, which is the foundation for the sound. Instead of hearing the mantra, you begin to feel the mantra as a vibration. After becoming skilled at this level, the vibration leads to complete, absolute silence. It is at this point that *samadhi*, the mystical experience, will be achieved. You experience the eternal nature of the spiritual Self consciously and directly and realize that your true identity is that of Divinity. In this moment, half the things that you worry about, half the fears of your mind, will disappear forever. You will no longer doubt the reality of the spiritual Self, even though you will not be able to sustain this experience. You have been taken to the mountaintop and have seen the promised land. Your quest now is to become skilled at regaining that experience.

For beginning a meditation using a mantra, I suggest the practice given below. The mantra *So Ham* (*Ham* is pronounced *hum*) is used in yoga as a training mantra. When you listen to the sound of your breath, you will hear "*so*" or "*sa*" on the inhalation and "*hum*" on the exhalation. Begin by focusing on the "*so*" with the inhalation and the "*hum*" with the exhalation. With every breath, you are confirming your own reality. Don't use *Ho Hum*—that will create a very different reality for your mind!

MANTRA MEDITATION

Begin this exercise seated in an erect posture with your eyes closed. For the first few moments, mentally scan the body, relaxing any tension you may find. Then, for a few minutes, practice breath awareness until you feel both nostrils open.

After a few moments, follow the next inhalation up as if you are following it into the center of your mind or down into the heart center, whichever is easier for you to focus on. The concentration should be on the space within the body, not on the surface. Now focus your attention on the sound of the breath. On the inhalation, you will hear the thought (sound) of *So*, on the exhalation the thought (sound) of *Ham*. Try to focus on exactly where the thought arises in your mind or heart center. Don't try to anticipate or remember, but stay focused on the thought itself as it exists in the moment. All sorts of thoughts will come to your mind. Let them come and go. Whenever you find your thoughts wandering or going off on a tangent, bring your attention back to the *So* and *Ham*. Don't struggle or fight with your mind; simply come back to the focus point.

At first, maintain the coordination of the thought with the movement of the breath—*So* on the inhalation, and *Ham* on the exhalation. Let the breath become very fine, very smooth and even. Then, after a few moments, let go of your awareness of the breath and focus only on the sound of the *So* and *Ham*. Concentrate on listening to the sound, not thinking about the sound.

Sit very still, maintaining this focus for as long as you comfortably can. When you are ready to finish, direct your attention to the flow of breath through the inner space of your body. Follow the next exhalation back up and out the nostrils, and focus your attention on the feeling of the breath for a few moments. Then gently wriggle your toes and fingers and slowly raise your hands to your face. Holding the hands next to each other, palms facing you, open your eyes to the palms of your hands. Maintain the inner calm and stillness you feel for as long as possible throughout the day.

So Ham is from Sanskrit, the language of the Vedas and other ancient Hindu scriptures of India. In sanskrit, *So Ham* is translated as "I am." It confirms Divinity as personal identity. Again, this does not mean that the personality, consisting of body, mind and habits, is Divine. The personality is part of the material world and exists totally within the realm of the ego-self. It specifically means that your true identity is that of the spiritual Self.

The great secret is that we don't have to become Divine; we need only to discover that seed of Divinity already within ourselves. This direct experience of the spiritual Self, and this realization alone, frees us from ignorance. According to an ancient saying, "A fool goes into deep sleep and emerges a fool. But when a fool enters *samadhi,* he emerges as a sage." This mystical experience forever loosens the grip of the ego. We no longer identify ourselves with the mind/body complex or see ourselves as only the personality. We experience that spark of Divinity as our own mystical Self, the same Self of all others. We realize that we are the Love of the spiritual Self. We are released from ignorance, and the limits of the ego-self no longer enslave us. This experience of "I and my Father are One" forever frees us from the grip of loneliness. One mystical experience loosens the chains of identity with the ego, but the habits of the mind are strong, and those chains are only loosened, not yet annihilated. Meditation does not end with *samadhi*—it only begins with it.

To realize the spiritual Self as true I-ness requires more than prayer, but prayer serves as powerful help on the journey. Prayer necessarily requires a belief in God, whereas meditation requires only a profound curiosity. Anyone can achieve *samadhi*, regardless of whether or not they believe in God. But if prayer is also used, then the process of meditation is enhanced, the discipline is acquired more rapidly and deeply and the final goal is achieved more quickly.

Self-realization, conscious ongoing awareness of the spiritual Self, requires the same honesty, commitment and surrender that prayer requires, as well as courage and strength. To penetrate the maze of the mind will demand every last bit of strength that you can muster. At times nature, culture, friends and family and, most important, your own mind will rise up against you and create seemingly insurmountable problems. An effective meditation practice causes the most difficult problems and greatest fears to surface in the mind. There may even be a time when you must be willing to die to reach your goal. Your strength, determination and capacity will be tested to the extreme. At such a time, the serenity of prayer is very helpful. During such crises, many turn aside from the journey, postponing their freedom and joy. They blame the teacher, they become discouraged or they give in to the habits, desires and fears of their mind. They find any excuse to stop the journey.

But if you persist, if you surrender the need to control, if you are willing to give up everything for that one realization—that final goal of spiritual Self-realization—then you will successfully meet and overcome these challenges. When you do so, you find even greater strength, joy and fulfillment. In a biblical parable, a man sells everything he has to acquire the one perfect pearl. This is the cost of spiritual knowledge. To be successful, you cannot simply practice a meditation technique once or twice a day. It must become your life. The spiritual Self is not a part-time reality, but the only Reality. To achieve the greatest state of knowledge requires the greatest effort.

CONTEMPLATION: THE FINAL JOURNEY

Through prayer, we discover the ecstasy of Amazing Grace. Through meditation, we discover that our true identity lies not in the ego-self but the spiritual Self, and we achieve Self-realization. Through contemplation, we discover that what we believe is the real world is only a temporary reality, one in which the only constants are change, death and decay. The only true Reality is one which that does not change. We refer to that one unchanging, eternal Reality as God. With the development of this insight, this inner vision, we literally begin to see the Divinity everywhere we look. We no longer experience the illusion of separation. Contemplation is the final step to complete realization of God and total freedom from loneliness.

Contemplation is the final refinement of the intellect. Through contemplation, the discrimination function of the mind becomes so powerful that it no longer mistakes the temporal world as the only reality. The intellect becomes like a perfect mirror, no longer distorted and colored by the senses and the material world. With the heart and mind purified by prayer and meditation, the intellect reflects the Divinity itself, and, everywhere we look, we see the omnipotence and omniscience of God. No matter who, what or where the apparent reality is before us, we see only the Divine. All duality—good and evil, right and wrong, heaven and hell, up and down and in and out—is resolved in this contemplation of Truth.

We are not at all out of touch with normal reality. In fact, we see the world around us with unsurpassed clarity and insight. But what we used to see as separate from ourselves is now only another aspect of the Divine, which is the spiritual Self. What we feared was God, what we ate was God, what we thought was God. We also see that every living creature is a presence of God, every nonliving thing is an expression of God, every action is an action of God. There is nowhere that God does not exist. We are no longer fooled by appearances, and we realize that life itself is the playground of God.

Of the three paths, contemplation is the most difficult. Both prayer and meditation are necessary if we want to become skilled in contemplation. Through prayer we learn to surrender to a higher power and loosen the control of the ego-self. Surrender is essential in contemplation, allowing us to strip away limiting belief systems in order to see clearly. Without the ability to let go of past beliefs, concepts and ideas, we can never go beyond our own conditioning. Meditation is necessary to develop and refine the power of concentration. Without the ability to focus attention, contemplation is nothing more than distracted reflection, full of competing thoughts, desires, fears and wants. Genuine contemplation can be accomplished only through intense concentration. Otherwise, it degenerates into mental masturbation, with little power to penetrate the vast, shadowy realm of the mind.

THE REFLECTIVE POWER OF PURE INTELLECT

In chapter 2 the four main functions of the mind were discussed: the sensory, memory, ego and discrimination functions. The sensory function, along with memory, creates the personal sense of reality out of the raw data of sensory input. We know that emotions, part of the sensory mind, can mislead us if not managed properly. We understand that the ego function creates the sense of separate personal identity that is the source of loneliness. And when we use the function of discrimination, we are able to analyze, make decisions and understand the world around us.

Discrimination is potentially the most powerful function of the mind. It is pure intellect, which has the power to acquire perfect knowledge and understanding. Even though it is within the scope of the ego-self, it is the only part of the mind with the capacity to reflect the truth of the spiritual Self. With the intellect we analyze data and make decisions. The intellect, or discriminating function, utilizes the sensory data collected and organized by the sensory function, but it is not limited by time/space and pain/pleasure which restrict the sensory function and build habits. Consequently, knowledge created by pure intellect is free from emotional distortion and the nearly automatic reactions that characterize habits. Because the intellect understands cause-effect relationships clearly, it has the power to understand future consequences.

The intellect has the power to see reality as it is, not as we wish, want or fear it to be, or as we have learned to see it. The more skillfully we apply this power of discrimination, the greater our insights and the more effective we will be in the world. Great insights and accomplishments are achieved because of intense focus and refined discrimination. It doesn't matter what the subject—art, science, mathematics, literature—it is the investment we spend in time and effort thinking about, studying and pondering a subject that produces great achievement.

But if we aren't careful with the way we think, we can be fooled by our mind. Our hopes, fears, desires and even our belief systems can distort how we think, make us see things that aren't there and believe in things that don't exist. Even more subtle is the power of our culture to determine how we think. We grow up in a certain way—as a white, American male, a black, South African female, a Vietnamese, a Christian, or Buddhist, or Jew, speaking English, Cantonese, Swahili— and each of these backgrounds shapes the mind in powerful ways, biasing the way we think. If we are to refine the intellect, we must find a way to go beyond the limits of our culture, belief systems and emotions. This is quite a task, to say the least.

To accomplish this requires that we strengthen the intellect. Learning how to think is only part of the answer. Logic is a helpful tool, but logic is only a methodology to minimize error. It is not the truth, it is a way to think. We must apply logic and reasoning, but with the full recognition that they are only tools and susceptible to error. The real key lies in our capacity to step outside of the mind to become a witness and observe the mind and its functions. Through meditation, we experience our identity as the spiritual Self, a reality distinct from the mind. At that moment, mind becomes an object of our awareness, and we can be completely objective about our own thoughts. If my identity remains locked inside the ego-self, there is no way I can observe how the mind works. Even if I analyze my mind, the very tool I use to analyze the mind is the mind itself. And the mind will do whatever is necessary to protect its own integrity and maintain its current structure.

The act of contemplation involves objective observation and rigorous discrimination. Nothing is accepted as fact or truth. The process is to discern relationships, not to reach conclusions. Good and bad become irrelevant; judgment is recognized as a trap for the mind. Categories are seen as temporary shelters, constructed only to facilitate further observation. In other words, the knowledge process of the mind remains entirely fluid, probing deeper and deeper into the nature of ideas, concepts, things and actions. Contemplation is not only thinking about something, but also focusing the whole mind, all attention, on the object of study. Our whole being—emotions, thoughts, actions—becomes involved.

This is not as strange as you might think. This is the same process by which a truly great scientist understands the material world. A true scientist holds no belief, no law, no construct as sacred. Even the so-called "laws of nature" are understood as simply useful constructs. Every belief is sacrificed in the quest for greater knowledge. All great scientific insights result from someone's ability to think more clearly about a topic than anyone else, to see relationships that previously had been ignored by others. The reality didn't change; only the capacity to understand it changed. The history of science is filled with the deaths of old beliefs and old facts. When a scientist loses the capacity to think beyond currently held belief systems, then he or she no longer acts as a true scientist. Instead, such scientists become guardians of the status quo. There is truth in the saying, "Science proceeds death by death." The older we get, the more rigidly we tend to hold on to beliefs. This rigidity reflects the ego-self, and it prevents us from accepting new knowledge. Younger scientists tend to be more open to change, more creative and more willing to challenge "accepted truth." They are less identified with the older concepts because their egos aren't involved with them. They are often more willing to entertain novel ways of seeing things. When the old guard dies out, new ideas come more easily into the mix, and reality is interpreted in a new way.

Few of us realize that we can use the power of discrimination that characterizes good science to gain insight into the spiritual Self and Divinity. Instead of contemplating and thinking about the world around us, the mystic directs the power of the intellect inward and explores the spiritual reality within. As his or her intellect is sharpened and strengthened through inner focus, he or she gains insight into the spiritual Self and the spiritual foundation of the world. Like the great scientist, the mystic becomes totally absorbed in the object of study.

In meditation, we focus on a single thought, image or sensation in order to refine our power of concentration. We keep returning to that single point of focus. But in contemplation, we focus on the relational aspects of the point of focus. For example, if I am contemplating the phrase "Jesus is Love," I would allow myself to experience every meaning it could possibly have. I would explore how it affects my behavior, my emotions, my thinking and my perceptions. I would not only think about every possible meaning of this phrase, but also I would identify with this phrase and experience every possible emotional state related to it. But I would not accept any one aspect as the final answer or reality. I would keep searching for an even deeper meaning, an even more subtle dimension.

In the great Vedic tradition of contemplation, no thought, label or construct is accepted as the final cause. It is the philosophy of negation—*nyeti, nyeti, nyeti*—meaning "not this, not this, not this." The power of discrimination is so refined that it finally leads one to recognize that even the names of God are only names. As a great yogi sage once said, "I had to take my sword and slay the Divine Mother." The sword was the power of discrimination, the Divine Mother was his concept of Divinity, his belief in God. With the power of discrimination, the great sage realized that his belief of God was not God, only a belief. Only by giving up the belief was he able to realize the actuality, the direct experience of God.

Through contemplation, all belief must be surrendered, all dogmas discarded, all concepts pushed until their unreality becomes apparent. Not a single knowledge state must remain held by the intellect as truth. It must be completely purified, through discrimination, of all belief. Through this negation of belief, we experience the pure truth of Existence.

This does not mean that we believe nothing, only that we recognize that beliefs are only beliefs or constructs to help us manage material reality effectively. Our belief systems should become ever more sophisticated, ever more supported by evidence, facts and direct experience. Without a belief system, we cannot move forward. But beliefs are vehicles to take us into our direct experience. They are not truth. Regardless of how many "facts" we gather, or how many others agree with us, beliefs are only beliefs, not reality itself. For instance, we can believe that we are hungry, but that will not motivate us to eat. When we feel hunger, then we take steps to acquire some food. All beliefs, no matter how sacred or profane, are only beliefs, not direct experience. Through contemplation, we train our mind to see beyond the belief into the realm of direct experience.

We have all changed beliefs as we gain knowledge. As children, we believed in certain things. But as we grew into adults, we learned that those beliefs were not true. As we grow in spiritual experience, our belief systems also undergo a change. This is natural. At one time everyone believed that the world was flat. The greatest, most learned minds of the time all agreed that the world was flat. But as human beings gained greater experience, the belief had to change. Many of us still believe that the only reality is material reality, that the only self is the ego-self of the personality. But as we refine our skills in prayer, meditation and contemplation, we will gain new and different experiences, and our belief systems will begin to change.

Beliefs can never satisfy our spiritual hunger, nor can they eliminate loneliness. Beliefs are structures of the mind, patterns of mind energy, and, as such, are part of the ego-self. Only when we surrender our beliefs, when we take our swords and destroy our concept of God, are we free to experience God directly. This takes great effort and persistence. The mind does not easily surrender its beliefs, habits, fears and desires. They must be pried from the mind, one by one, and surrendered to the purifying flame of direct experience.

BEGINNING THE PRACTICE OF
CONTEMPLATION

We begin this aspect of our journey with experimentation. Like meditation, contemplation requires guidance from an accomplished master. However, as in all spiritual practices, if you begin with sincerity and commitment, put your heart into your journey with prayer and cleanse and calm the mind with meditation, then your beginning practice of contemplation will begin to bear fruit. Sooner or later, the guidance will appear when you are ready for it.

There are a number of experiments that you can do to explore contemplation. The first is a very active process: for a period of one month, don't say anything that you don't absolutely believe to be true. This means you can't exaggerate, you can't do or say something you really don't want to do or say, and you must answer questions truthfully and honestly or not at all. For thirty days, be absolutely certain of everything you say. That doesn't mean you won't make mistakes or find out later that something you said was inaccurate. It only means that when you say something, you are saying it with absolute integrity. You believe it to be absolutely true.

Carefully observe the situations in which you want to say something but hold back because you are not sure if it's true. Be aware of your difficulties with this task and the times when you slip and say something that you really don't believe. How do all of these situations affect you? What happens to your conversations at work or at home? How do you feel when you stop yourself from saying something you aren't absolutely sure of?

After thirty days, take an evening to evaluate what happened. How do you feel about the experiment? What did you learn about yourself and others? What effect did the experiment have on your relationships at home and at work? Do you want to continue with this practice, or is it a relief to stop it?

After doing this exercise, choose a spiritual phrase that is meaningful to you. Then apply that phrase to your everyday life. For instance, you might select the phrase "God is Love." What does that mean to you as you interact with others? Does keeping that phrase in the forefront of your mind change how you react to other people? How does it change the way you work? How does it change the way you commute? What changes, if any, occur in your day-to-day life when you act as if the phrase were actually true? What happens to your emotions? What does it make you think about? Keep track of your thoughts and experiences in a daily log. Don't just write down what you do or what happens to you, but write what you felt, what your thoughts were and even what happened to the quality of your sleep. Try to see how this one thought influences every aspect of your daily life.

People skilled in contemplation will spend months, even years concentrating on a single contemplative point. The goal is always to expand insight and wisdom, to see more deeply and clearly into the nature of that truth. There is a great deal of material to use as a source of contemplation: scriptures, ethical truths, ideals. But whatever is chosen as a contemplative point should have a positive spiritual or ethical meaning to you. As you become more skilled, the insights become more penetrating and the wisdom more complete.

PUTTING IT ALL TOGETHER

We are all on a spiritual journey whether we recognize it or not. If God is omniscient and omnipotent, as every religion says, then God is the journey. The task is to consciously recognize that we are part of this Divinity and to learn how to make that Divinity a conscious part of our everyday life. As I wrote in an earlier book, we are not here as human beings to have a spiritual experience, but we are here as spiritual beings here to have a human experience. When we ignore that fundamental reality of our spiritual Self, we suffer enormously. As long as we remain identified with the ego-self, we will suffer from the emotional disturbances generated by fear and self-hatred, and we will never solve the problem of loneliness.

We need not become an expert in prayer, meditation and contemplation, but we should become skilled in at least one of these three paths. We also need to practice the other two even though our primary effort will be toward one. For example, prayer is the easiest, most accessible of the three paths. Many, particularly those in the West, do not have the understanding, technical facility, or cultural interest to pursue meditation or contemplation. Since they are not yet an integral part of Western culture, meditation and contemplation often seem difficult and arduous.

But even those who prefer prayer will benefit enormously from practicing meditation and contemplation. Even a small, limited practice of these two powerful tools leads to greater understanding and enhanced self-mastery. Both contemplation and meditation make prayer more effective. These two tools enhance the ability to listen closely. Everyone wants to talk to God, but few are willing to listen deeply. Meditation is the art of listening deeply, as well as the systematic process of mystical Self-discovery, and contemplation makes us more aware of the reality of God that surrounds us.

These three spiritual practices develop the awareness of our inner strength, which allows us to perfect nonattachment. Without inner strength, nonattachment becomes an escape mechanism, a way to avoid responsibilities and choices. Without inner strength, nonattachment is not possible, and we remain dependent on the objects of the world. Then, loneliness is endless and unresolvable.

But more important, these practices lead to the complete realization of the spiritual Self within ourselves and within all others. Like the great sage in the parable that opened this chapter, we become the Love that constitutes the spiritual Self. We finally realize that "My Father and I are One." Through prayer, meditation and contemplation, we fulfill our spiritual heritage and achieve real freedom.

CHAPTER 5

SELFLESS SERVICE: LOVE IN ACTION

The practice of love is the natural awareness of God.

WE PRAY, meditate and contemplate in order to become aware of the spiritual Self within and to experience the Divine. But these three paths do not exist in a vacuum. They affect, and are affected by, the lifestyle we lead. We can pray fervently, meditate intensely and contemplate deeply every day. But if we are egotistical and selfish in our daily life, it's going to take a very long time before even these powerful tools can transform the personality. What we do every day has an enormous impact on us. If our emotional reactions are out of control, if we constantly feed the ego-self, we not only slow our journey to freedom, but also make it tortuous and miserable for everyone, including ourselves.

A spiritual journey requires more than tithing ten percent of our income, more than weekly meetings at a church, mosque or synagogue, more than giving money to charity. Love, not emotional attachment, must be the signature of our lifestyle. It must permeate every aspect of life, from the most mundane to the most esoteric. If we want to experience the presence of God, then how we live must reflect that spiritual Reality. What benefit do we achieve if we spend fifteen minutes twice a day cleaning our mind through meditation and then spend the other twenty-three and a half hours making it dirty again? How helpful is it to pray for world peace and then emotionally abuse our spouse, children or colleagues? And what can we gain by spending an hour every day contemplating great truths if we spend our work life trying to find ways to take advantage of others?

Of course, whatever time we spend on a spiritual practice benefits us. But we should appreciate how difficult it is to gain freedom from loneliness, and other dragons created by the ego-self, when we spend ninety percent of our time reinforcing the ego-self and only ten percent strengthening spiritual awareness. If we want to successfully free ourselves from the grip of the ego-self and the loneliness it creates, we must create a lifestyle that supports this goal instead of one which makes it more difficult.

It isn't so much *what* we do as *how* we go about it. If we choose to support ourselves by intentionally doing things that harm others, our spiritual development will certainly suffer. A lifestyle of crime and terror against others only reinforces the worst qualities of the ego-self and strengthens the fear, self-hatred and loneliness that we suffer. If we live life with fear and violence, then we will suffer fear and violence.

On the other hand, we don't have to become religious fanatics, monks or clerics. To live a life dedicated to love and spiritual awareness, it isn't necessary to dedicate our life to the poor in Calcutta or run soup kitchens in New York City. The secret isn't what we do, but how much love we bring to the things we do. Work, home life, play, leisure time—everything we do provides opportunities to practice loving and to free ourselves from emotional disturbances, from fear and worry, from self-hatred and from the illusion of loneliness. Selfless love is the hidden power of life, the only true freedom from the suffering and pain that characterize the world of the ego-self. By loving others, as well as ourselves, we not only put an end to our own misery, but also help others become free from theirs.

SELFLESS SERVICE: THE PRINCESS AND THE NUN

In 1997, within the space of just a few days, two very remarkable women died. They couldn't have been in greater contrast to each other.

Princess Diana, a beautiful thirty-six-year-old woman, the ex-wife of the future king of England and mother of two princes, was a woman who learned through bitter experience to set her own agenda. She was born into a wealthy family, married Prince Charles, became a fashion plate who traveled in the wealthiest social circles, and was a media star. She personified beauty and vulnerability. In a sense, she became a screen onto which millions of women projected their longings. Although her funeral was attended by movies stars and royalty, she was known as the "people's princess," and the streets were lined with millions of ordinary people who wished to pay their respects to her.

The other was born of European peasant stock, was never married and spent most of her life in the slums of Calcutta. Mother Teresa was a nun who dedicated her life to voluntary poverty and serving the poor. She was not photogenic, and she did not achieve star status in the media. No movie stars came to her funeral, and no rock stars dedicated songs to her. Rather, she was a stern woman of definite beliefs and ethics. But her dedication to serving the most miserable of the poor earned her the love and respect of millions, as well as a Nobel Peace Prize. Her casket was driven to the church in a van, her funeral was attended by fellow nuns, and the streets of Calcutta were lined with millions of poor and ordinary people who wished to honor her life.

These two famous women, dying within days of each other, lived very different lives and walked very different paths. Interestingly, they knew each other. Princess Diana was an admirer of Mother Teresa; she gained inspiration from the nun for her own fund-raising efforts to support children and charities. In return, Mother Teresa admired Diana's dedication to raising money for charity, her work with children and lepers, and her independent spirit. When she heard of Princess Diana's death, Mother Teresa was reported to have said "What a beautiful, sad woman." Only a few days later, Mother Teresa herself died.

As different as they were, these two incredible women shared a power born of their dedication to serve others. Diana began as a kindergarten teacher and ended up marrying a prince. The marriage was a dismal failure, and Diana's initial reaction was to become anorexic and suicidal. But somehow she began to open her heart, using her status and position to raise money for charities that served people that most of society shunned. Her genuine concern and dedication to alleviate suffering gave her strength, joy and recognition that she had never found in her disastrous marriage and jetset life. This simple act of love—opening her heart to serve others—gave life back to Diana.

And yet personal happiness somehow eluded her. She was unable to bring that selfless love, which she so readily shared with others, into her personal life, and she continued to suffer disappointment and unhappiness. She was famous for her vulnerability and unhappiness as well as for her charity work. Her attachment to the material world was too great, and she never found the contentment she desperately sought.

Mother Teresa was respected for her complete devotion to service. She showed the integrity of pure love. There was no vulnerability in this old woman—only a strength that, particularly in her later years, made her physical weaknesses seem totally irrelevant. This frail, eighty-seven-year-old woman was a power that could not be resisted. It was not the power of media attention, beauty, royalty or wealth. Her determination arose out of her love and her simple faith. Her spiritual practices of prayer and silence formed a powerful tool in developing her inner strength. As Mother Teresa put it, "The fruit of silence is prayer; the fruit of prayer is faith; the fruit of faith is love; the fruit of love is service."

Those who knew her spoke of her strength, determination and unswerving dedication to her mission. But they also spoke of the joy that characterized her every moment, the love of life that she brought to her work and to those around her. No one would ever say of her, "What a beautiful, sad woman." Father Andrew Greeley wrote that Mother Teresa was "radiantly happy . . . she was the happiest human being I had ever met." He recognized that it wasn't her work with the poor that made her a saint in people's eyes, but her unstinting devotion to unselfishness. This selfless love, which flows from the spiritual Self, created her happiness and joy, and her love found its natural expression in service.

Mother Teresa wasn't a perfect person, nor was Princess Diana. They both made mistakes, but these were easily forgiven and forgotten, irrelevant in the light of their love and unselfishness. Their capacity for selfless love earned them the respect and love of millions. It isn't a matter of serving the poor, raising money for charities or any other particular thing we do. Our only task is to learn selfless love, to reach into our spiritual core and to be the love that we already are.

LOVE AS A LIFESTYLE

Learning to be selfless isn't easy in a materially-oriented culture that emphasizes fortune and fame as the highest ideals of life. We are constantly bombarded with messages to buy this and acquire that. If we only lived in this neighborhood, drove that kind of car, had this level of income, had the right plastic surgery, had brilliant children educated at an Ivy League school, ate nonfat food, had the right exercise equipment, etc., etc., etc., then everything would be perfect and we would be forever happy.

To our dismay, fame and fortune are no guarantee of contentment and well-being. We live in the richest, most powerful country in the world. Yet, we have the highest rates of homelessness, crime and people in prison in the "civilized" world. Our murder rate is the highest in the world. Homelessness is a common reality in our cities. By contrast, Nepal is one of the poorest countries of the world, and the Nepalese work hard every day just to secure enough food to eat. But in Nepal, everyone has a home to live in.

The more wealth or fame we have, the more fearful we will be of losing both. We become more isolated from each other, afraid that someone will take our things away from us. After all, how can we share our wealth without lowering our standard of living? The more fearful we are, the greedier we become. We become more self-centered, less capable of loving and more dependent on the objects of our desires. The materialism we create becomes a vicious circle, leading only to greater insecurity and unhappiness as we slowly become more and more centered around the ego. We become more isolated from the true power of our own humanity, the selfless love of the spiritual Self.

Achieving bliss, joy and contentment has never really depended on things or on other people's opinions. We simply need to examine our own experience to confirm this. To realize what is most important to you, and to become aware of the source of your happiness, do the following exercise very seriously.

You have just been told you have a fatal illness and only ten days left to live. There are no remarkable cures, no miracles. But you do have all the resources (except time) to do whatever you want to do in those ten days. Take fifteen minutes to think about how you will spend these last ten days. Get a clean piece of paper and a pen and write out what you will do, how you will spend your time, and with whom.

Now read back to yourself what you have written. How did you choose to spend your time and why? What personal values emerge from this exercise? What is really important to you? What seemed to matter most to you? What would you do during that last ten days of your life to create the most joy and contentment?

Then, take another clean piece of paper and write down whatever wisdom you wish to communicate to those you leave behind. What piece of advice, wisdom or truth would you like others—your children, your spouse, your friends—to have as a legacy of your own experiences, knowledge and wisdom? Write this clearly and legibly, so if anyone picks up this piece of paper, he or she can easily read the pearls of wisdom that you have gleaned from life.

When you have finished, read what you have written aloud to yourself. Are you following your own wisdom? Is what you have written the real focus of your life, or are you distracted by obtaining things? Do you really live what you already know is the re[...] of life?

Keep this piece of paper by your desk. Look at it at lea[...] every day. At night, take a few minutes and review what you have done during the day. Did you follow your own advice? Did you become pre-occupied with the struggles of making a living, or did you also find time and space to practice loving others?

When we do this exercise in my seminars, no one ever writes that he or she wants to earn at least one more percentage point on his investments, spend more time creating profit or buy an expensive car. Universally, the participants talk about the love they want to express to their family and friends—they want to make amends in their relationships, spend time in nature, prayer and solitude, share whatever they can with others and celebrate their lives. Permeating everything is the love they want to share with others. No one seems to be concerned about the love they get, but only what they can give. What does this say about love and the purpose of life? What does it tell us about joy and contentment? You see, what really counts is not life's material blessings, but the love we experience. And it is not the love we get from others, but the love we give that is most meaningful.

LOVE: THE PRACTICAL WAY OF LIFE

Some say that selfless love is not practical, that only the strong (meaning hard and mean) are successful. But, of all the successful people you know, how many are truly happy? How many are free from the dragons of fear and self-hatred? How many are truly free from the pangs of loneliness?

Selfless love is the most practical way of life. When we practice selflessness, we defuse fears, self-hatred and loneliness, and enjoy the freedom to express ourselves, to create, to think clearly and to focus on solving problems. Life becomes a joyful dance in which we share our unique individuality with others. What is more practical than that?

Some people combine thousands of single acts to make selfless love a lifestyle. In a rare moment in politics, President Bush inaugurated the Thousand Points of Light program to recognize individuals throughout America who were dedicated to helping others. One of the Points of Light was Elizabeth O'Donnell. She didn't start out to be a hero. All she wanted to do was ice-skate. But to thousands of handicapped children and their parents, she is a genuine hero. By age seventeen, Elizabeth joined the Ice Capades as its youngest member, and, in 1978, she ranked tenth in the world professional figure-skating championships. The romance of constant travel paled after two seasons, and she returned to Buffalo, New York, to teach private lessons. She loved teaching but found it lacked challenge. Then inspiration hit, and she decided to teach the blind.

At first, Elizabeth relied on visual communication, trying to show each person what to do. Her first class with blind students was nearly a disaster. After they left, Elizabeth closed her eyes and stepped out onto the ice . . . blind. Feeling awkward and uncoordinated, she experienced at least part of what the blind kids felt. Over and over she stepped out onto the ice, discovering at last a "blind" way to feel the grace, freedom and trust in her body that she knew was possible.

In the second lesson, Elizabeth had her students sit on the ice. "Touch it, feel it with your hands," she told them. "Feel how you can slide." She had them touch their skates, "seeing" the steel tips with their finger tips. Then she stood them up. They had so much fun, she couldn't get them off the ice.

This uncanny ability to empathize and communicate with handicapped children didn't stop there. For months, Elizabeth struggled to convince the community that it was possible for people with disabilities to ice-skate. Despite negative feedback, Elizabeth continued her crusade, and, in March 1977, her persistence and determination paid off. What was once a dream became a reality. The Skating Association for the Blind and Handicapped—SABAH—was formally incorporated as a not-for-profit educational corporation. SABAH's sole purpose is to provide individuals who are physically, mentally or emotionally challenged the opportunity to reach their fullest potential through the development of ice-skating skills and the opportunity to perform in an annual skating spectacular.

SABAH skaters range in age from sixteen months to seventy-three years. Each skater's challenge is unique and requires specialized training and equipment. But the key to their success is the love and direction that Elizabeth provides.

There was Eddy, a two-year-old with Down's syndrome who doctors said wouldn't walk until he was eight. Elizabeth put him on the ice, and in eight weeks he was walking! Then there was Leslie, a young girl born with spastic cerebral palsy who progressed from wheelchair to walkers to crutches. Eventually, she was able to walk unaided for the first time because of the strength and balance she developed through ice-skating.

The benefits of the program reach the whole community. Elizabeth remembers three high-school boys, "macho" hockey players, who volunteered to help. She assigned them to work with Kristin, an eight-year-old who is so disabled she cannot speak. At first, Kristin needed all three boys to hold her up. Then she could skate with only two helpers, the third skated backward in front of her, cheering her on. She quickly progressed to where she only needed to hold the hands of the two boys, and then one. Within weeks, the boys were forming a triangle, and Kristin would skate from one to the next, each time receiving a hug. "I couldn't tell you who got more out of it—Kristin or the boys," said Elizabeth.

Since 1977, Elizabeth and the volunteers of SABAH have taught over 8,000 challenged children and adults. Elizabeth has earned many honors, but when you listen to her talk, you never hear of her awards and achievements. You only hear about a special child she is working with. In her voice is admiration for the child's courage and her love for that child. She recognizes that the real heroes are the brave kids who face their handicaps and achieve the freedom, grace and trust in their bodies that learning to skate provides.

Elizabeth's entire philosophy of life can be summed up in one word: *service*. Dedicated to the children and adults who come to SABAH, Elizabeth demands and receives the same dedication to service from her staff and the volunteers. She is one of the most positive, joyful and energetic individuals you could ever hope to meet. Her commitment to children supports her own spiritual practices of prayer and meditation. We find this joy whenever we become selfless, whenever we forget about our own small selves and dedicate our efforts to benefit others.

THE SIMPLICITY OF SELFLESS LOVE

"Wait a minute," you say. "Not everyone can help the handicapped, just as everyone can't be serving the poor. What about a typical lifestyle—one that involves raising and providing for a family, paying the bills, going to work every day, taking care of a house—how does selfless service fit into a normal person's life? How can I create a spiritual journey out of my normal life?"

This isn't as difficult as you might think. Selfless service comes from the heart, not from what you do. Being selfless means that you do your duties with as much skill as you can without being concerned about what you will get in return. It means that you don't put your own wants before the needs of others. In other words, you simply practice loving others. Those others are every person that you meet in life—children, spouse, co-workers, neighbors. You don't have to travel the world to find opportunities to serve others. They are right in front of you all the time.

There are many ways to express love: listening attentively to a child, providing a warm, safe and comfortable home for your family, disciplining a teenager, helping a co-worker solve a problem. Love is not a particular action nor is it passiveness in the face of hostility or aggression. Love is the expression of the spiritual Self, a way of being in the world that minimizes the demands of the ego. When you focus on serving others to the best of your ability, you forget about your own self-created miseries. If you aren't concerned with your own miseries, you are free to experience the joy of that self-expression. Selfless love is always an act of joy.

When you forget your ills and worries to help someone else, then you are loving. When you refuse to facilitate someone else's dependencies, then you are loving. At any moment, love may be as gentle as a spring rain or as hard as a diamond. It is accommodating and demanding, but never for its own benefit. As the force behind SABAH, Elizabeth is a successful leader and a fearless fund-raiser because she isn't doing it for herself; she is doing it for the children.

Selfless love begins with yourself—not the self-centered, indulgent self-love of pop psychology, but the experience of being love itself. It involves respect for the mind and body as the finest tools we have. All good craftsmen respect their tools. They take care of them and keep them in good shape, ready for whatever task is next. We should do the same with the mind and body, the tools that constitute the personality. We respect and love the body when we feed it healthy food, give it the exercise it needs and protect it from the elements. Our bodies become healthy and strong with proper breathing, diet and exercise, prepared for whatever tasks we ask of them and free from unnecessary stress and disease.

We respect and love our minds when we learn emotional control and self-discipline to minimize bad habits such as fear, self-hatred and negative thinking. Just as we feed our bodies healthy food, we must feed our minds with healthy mental food. Read books that open positive new possibilities rather than unhealthy desires. Watch movies and plays that inspire us rather than play on the base emotions of fear and revenge. Focus on participation, team play and enjoyment rather than beating others at all costs. Competition is healthy when it celebrates effort and performance rather than winning and being number one.

Love arises out of the Spirit-center, not the ego-center. But love also means that we respect the ego-self as a proper tool and treat it as such. Our personalities should sparkle with unique qualities and strengths. We should be all that we can be, but always in the service of the spiritual Self, not the ego. Genuine self-love is created through self-discipline and self-knowledge and is characterized by self-respect.

Notice the suggestion to *practice* loving others. The task is not to become "perfect," whatever that might mean. Patience, practice and persistence are the keys. All people—great and not so great—make mistakes. Mistakes are opportunities to learn. Our task is not to become more godlike. The core spiritual Self is already a spark of the Divine. God cannot become more godlike. Nor do we need to improve upon or conquer Mother Nature. Our task is to successfully blend these two and become fully human. We don't have to achieve perfection; we simply must become who we already are.

Too many of us mistakenly think that the human being is smarter than God and Nature. This arrogance creates both personal and social problems, such as environmental disasters. The continuing advances in genetics could pose even more serious problems, especially if we fail to think clearly, compassionately and spiritually about what we create. Curiosity and intelligence are powerful tools in the quest for knowledge, but egocentric arrogance only leads to disaster. We don't need to conquer Nature, we need to understand its subtleties. If we are in touch with our spiritual Self, wisdom, instead of arrogance, will guide our decisions.

HUMILITY: THE ANTIDOTE TO ARROGANCE

Humility is the greatest friend we have. It is also the antidote to human arrogance. When we practice humility, we practice loving. But unfortunately, humility is generally not understood. We confuse it with being a doormat and letting others walk all over us, allowing others to impose their beliefs and values on us, or denying our strengths and capacities. Humility is none of these things. These serious affronts to our integrity as human beings should not be accepted or allowed under any circumstances.

Genuine humility is quite different. It is the recognition and over-powering sense of awe when we realize that we are a small part of something much greater than ourselves. We have all felt this humility. Think of a clear, dark night when, away from all artificial lights, you lay on your back looking at the stars. For most of us, this powerful experience shows us that we are a small but integral part of a vast uni-verse. Many of us feel this awe when we participate in the birth of a child. Something similar happens when we listen to an extraordinary concert and everyone feels the magic of the shared experience of the music. The sense of awe that we experience is humility.

These experiences are powerful, and we remember them vividly. At these times, we listen to each other and we learn from each other. The ego's need to assert its individuality and superiority is diminished, and we relate to each other as brother and sister, as fellow sojourners on this wonderful journey called life. We feel strong, connected and wonderful. In short, we experience humility.

There are a number of traditional ways to discipline the ego and establish genuine humility—placing yourself in the position of a stu-dent with a master craftsman, learning martial arts, studying with a great teacher. Working with various agencies for the benefit of oth-ers—the Red Cross, Habitat for Humanity, The Sierra Club—is a wonderful way to gain the benefits of humility. These efforts gradu-ally train the ego to value service and learning, allowing a healthy, strong ego to develop—one that doesn't need to always assert itself as "Number One!"

Humility protects us from the dangers of fanaticism—a passion-ately narrow-minded insistence that one group of people alone knows the only truth, that its way of doing things is the only way, that its belief system is alone correct. Fanaticism reinforces the weaknesses of the ego and makes the ego-self more difficult to escape. The spiritual Self is contrary to fanaticism, whether of a political, religious or moral nature.

THE FIVE PRINCIPLES OF HARMONY

If we try always to be nice, we are living a lie. Selfless love isn't accomplished by always being nice or by going around hugging everyone. Selfless love is characterized by genuine self-confidence, independence and inner strength, not some sappy "everyone gets a hug" communalism. Great sages are powerful individuals; they are eagles and lions, not sparrows and cows. Selfless people don't act like wimps, but like bearers of the power of the Divine.

We access this strength through self-knowledge and self-discipline. We already have three powerful tools: prayer, meditation and contemplation. But why not live this strength day to day, moment to moment? We can make humility, that sense of awe, Amazing Grace, clarity and understanding a constant part of our life. We can become truly loving, selfless human beings and free ourselves from the terrible anxieties of loneliness. We can learn to live with harmony, integrity and honesty with ourselves and with the world around us.

Five principles are involved in becoming selfless: nonviolence, truthfulness, nonpossessiveness, sensory control and nonstealing. They provide the foundation for a spiritual lifestyle. These five principles serve as internal guidelines and practices to create inner harmony and a mind that is peaceful, unafraid and content. At the same time, we create an external environment characterized by respect, harmony and tranquillity in which challenge, opportunity and success can all thrive.

NONVIOLENCE: THE ART OF SKILLFUL LIVING

The first and foremost of these principles is nonviolence in thought, word and deed. Nonviolence means nonharming. We often confuse nonviolence with passivity and weakness, just as we confuse violence with being forceful. Being violent may involve power, but it has nothing to do with inner strength. In fact, it is just the opposite. Violence is not the use of force, but the overuse of force. We overuse power and force when we are fearful, imbalanced or weak. At the heart of all violence is fear. If we become fearless, we have no need to use violence or to take advantage of others.

The foundation for nonviolence is inner strength. If we don't live with strength—unless we know how to use and express force—the world will impose violence on us, and we should never allow that. Practicing nonviolence doesn't mean that we become passive in the face of adversity or wrong, that we submit to any attack, or that we do not stand firm for our beliefs and principles. If we have inner strength, we can stand up to any adversity and still maintain our humanity.

We cannot legislate nonviolence or make people be nonviolent. We can pass laws and punish people for being violent, but that, in itself, only leads to more violence. Our prisons are already reservoirs of violence and have become training grounds for further tragedy. Religions have failed to create a nonviolent society. In fact, religion has been one of the major causes of war, strife and murder.

Nonviolence is, first and foremost, a personal issue. As we practice meditation and become more sensitive to the nature of the mind, we slowly become aware that all actions are created first in the mind. Even emotional reactions are created there first. Before we start yelling at our spouse or children, some thought process creates the emotional reaction. The mind is the original source of all behaviors. If I want to harm you, I must first create that same condition within my own mind. Before I strike you and cause you pain, I must create that pain within my own mind. In other words, when I am violent, the first person to suffer is me. Nonviolence also begins within each individual mind. If I don't create that violence in my own mind, I cannot be violent in my behavior.

Violence also distorts clarity of thought, and we become much less effective in whatever we do. For example, when we don't get what we want or think we should have, we become angry. If our frustration boils over and we lose control, we often act in ways we later regret. When the mind suffers from violence, we lose the capacity to discriminate, to think clearly. We become more rigid in our behavior and less capable of solving problems. This only makes the ego-self stronger and more in control. Instead of expanding our identity, uncontrolled anger and violence makes us narrower.

Most important, when we harm others, we are really harming ourselves. As we become skilled in prayer, meditation and contemplation, we realize that the spiritual Self is the same Self in all beings. We are connected to each other in the most profound and spiritual way. We are more than brothers and sisters. On the spiritual level, we are one and the same Self. When we harm each other, we are literally harming ourselves. Just because we aren't aware of this principle doesn't mean it doesn't exist. It simply means that we are not yet fully conscious, not yet fully human. As we realize this spiritual truth through the mystical experience, we will be no longer capable of harming each other.

Arguably, one of the greatest practitioners of nonviolence was Mohandas K. Gandhi. His love and spiritual knowledge were so great that he overcame fear. Thus, he could lead the people of India to freedom from foreign rule without resorting to violence. Since his mind was free from fear and the distortions of violence, he saw clearly how to advance his objectives. No matter what the British did, Gandhi would find a way to use their behavior to benefit his cause. If they arrested him, he used it to his benefit. If they didn't arrest him, he used that to his benefit. When the Hindus and Muslims fought each other, he used his own body as a sacrifice to influence the events and stop the killing. Gandhi never responded to violence with violence. He remained clear-minded, focused on his goals and dedicated to nonviolence. This reinforced his enormous capacity to love and made his movement irresistible.

We are saddened and bewildered by how much violence we find in our cities, our communities, even our schools. And yet, we unknowingly glorify violence in our culture. We use fear to achieve monetary gain and economic and political power, and violence is a favorite form of entertainment. Just consider the consequences of the following facts. The United States is the leading manufacturer and seller of weapons. Americans insist on the freedom to carry a gun and have established politically powerful organizations to maintain that right. We license doctors, pharmacists, motor vehicle drivers, even beauticians but allow anyone, at any time, to buy a weapon. In a sense, we literally argue for a constitutional right to violence. This is not about hunting or sports. This is about fear. We allow television shows to glorify violence, feeding our minds, and those of our children, a daily dose of mayhem and killing. Violence is a sellable product. It increases ratings, sells newspapers and gains attention. The media does not "report" violence, but actively exploits it for monetary gain.

Whatever we feed the mind, we create in the mind and in our lives. Violence is a product of the ego-self, not the spiritual Self. The idea of a "holy war" is a complete distortion, the product of a disturbed mind. Violence can never be spiritual. It is, pure and simple, the distorted product of the ego-self and only serves to reinforce fears and hatreds.

Obvious violence, such as war, terrorism and the crimes of street gangs, is only the tip of the iceberg. A more subtle form is the violence we do in the name of profit. We build productivity and profits on unpaid overtime, poor working conditions, even child labor. Child labor is illegal in this country, so corporations go overseas to exploit foreign labor, including children. This is an act of violence. To justify this behavior by claiming that these children need the money cannot whitewash the greed that is the real motivation. Forcing people to work overtime without pay is an act of violence. Demanding that people sacrifice family and community for career and greater productivity is an act of violence. Selling products that are destructive, addictive and harmful, whether they are television shows, cigarettes or alcohol, is an act of violence. Poisoning the air and water, depleting natural resources and creating unlivable conditions for migrant workers are acts of violence. Violence follows quickly on the heels of greed.

Commerce, the honest exchange of products and services, is not inherently violent. There is nothing inherently wrong about making a profit. Business can be and should be a creative, life-enhancing endeavor. But when greed takes over, it becomes easy to make excuses for abusing others, taking advantage of others and promoting the use of destructive products. Commerce motivated by greed becomes harmful to others, to the communities in which we live—and to the perpetrators. We are acting out of fear and reinforcing the ego-self. So-called "trickle-down economics" is an argument for greed, resulting in greater isolation between those who benefit from business and those whom the trickle never reaches. The real outcome of this isolation is greater fear and loneliness.

Nonviolence is not an easy goal to achieve, nor is it a popular cause. We cannot wait for others to put an end to violence. We must begin with ourselves. As Gandhi once said, "You must be the change you wish to see in the world." The spiritual practices of prayer, meditation and contemplation will lead to inner strength. But we must also practice nonharming behaviors in practical ways every day. We begin with small things—giving up gossiping, practicing breath awareness to gain control over emotional reactions, refusing to support unsportsmanlike behavior whether acted out by Dennis Rodman or the local high-school basketball coach who puts winning above fair play, turning off television programs that use violence to capture attention, getting involved with the community and promoting healthy activities for its children.

Sports can be a wonderful way to train the mind and body, and it can be a powerful tool to teach nonviolence. Genuine sportsmanship is a great tool for personal development. Athletes can be wonderful models of self-expression and self-development. But when we glorify egotism in sports, it becomes violent. Decent sportsmanship and behavior are replaced with hostile aggressiveness. Some stars with "attitude" refuse to shake hands when they lose, and professional ice hockey has more to do with intimidation and brawling than skating. Money and greed become the driving forces. Dennis Rodman is a product of our culture, not an aberration.

We must recapture sports from the jaws of greed and re-create the ideal of sportsmanship. We must teach our children that the sheer joy of doing their best, not winning and losing, is the true purpose of sports.

One of the best ways to train the mind in nonviolence is through traditional martial arts. The purpose of martial arts is the development of self-knowledge, self-respect and spiritual awareness. The goal is complete fearlessness, because the martial artist recognizes that fear is the source of violence. The more fearless we become, the less violent we will be, and the more we will recognize the Divinity within each human being. If the martial artist is forced to fight, he or she will do so without fear. A skilled martial artist will use the other person's force to create a condition in which the attacker can no longer continue the attack. He or she always respects the Divinity within the opponent, even when the opponent is a genuine villain.

Nonviolence begins with each and every one of us. If nonviolence does not become a personal goal and accomplishment of many people, then we will never see it in our communities. It's not necessary to pass law after law, attempting to force others to be nonviolent. These won't work anyway. As Gandhi said, we must be the example; we must be the change we want to see in others. As we achieve greater skill in nonviolence, then others around us will benefit and begin to get the picture.

NONLYING: THE POWER OF PERSONAL INTEGRITY

The second principle is nonlying, or truthfulness. Truthfulness is the second principle because truth should never be used to intentionally harm others. When truth cannot be told without harming, then silence is often the best response. Sometimes, facing the truth is painful and difficult. But difficulty and pain don't necessarily result in harm. We will always have to decide when to be open and honest and when to be silent. And we will make mistakes. But if we use the principle of nonviolence as the guide for truthfulness, then truth will always benefit others as well as ourselves.

When actions and thoughts are guided by selflessness, the application of truthfulness becomes simple. Basically, we lie because we are afraid of losing something important to us or not gaining something we think we must have to be happy, content or secure. It may be affection, the respect of others, material gain, reputation, position—the list can be endless. But as we grow in our capacity to be selfless, to be spirit-centered rather than ego-centered, we also grow in our capacity to use truthfulness properly and with wisdom. We will know when to speak up and when to remain silent.

The power of truthfulness is reflected in the biblical phrase "The truth shall set you free." This is no great hidden secret, to be uncovered in some yet undiscovered ancient manuscript. This living reality is right before our eyes and affects every dimension and aspect of life. At the most profound spiritual level, it speaks of ignorance and the reality of the spiritual Self. But it is equally relevant to the most mundane details of life.

Being truthful with ourselves is sometimes difficult. In earlier chapters, we saw how habits really regulate most of what we think and do. Habits function because they are part of the unconscious mind. But the moment we become aware of what we are thinking or doing, we can change what we think or do. The greater my self-awareness, the easier it is to free myself from unwanted and destructive thoughts and behaviors. Knowing the truth of who I am and how habits are limiting me gives me the freedom to think and act more constructively.

Our spiritual growth demands that we be totally honest with ourselves. But being honest doesn't mean being judgmental. It simply requires that we recognize when we are truthful with ourselves and when we aren't. This simple act of discrimination allows us to gain greater self-awareness which, in turn, gives us the freedom to express ourselves through our choices and to develop into the kind of person we really want to be.

We are untruthful with ourselves for the same reasons we are untruthful with others: we are afraid of facing the truth. Unfortunately, we end up living in the superficial images of who we think we are supposed to be—images we learned as children—rather than who we actually are. Too many of us never gain the self-awareness necessary to really understand ourselves or appreciate our unique qualities. We can't develop our strengths because we aren't aware of them. Isolated from our true qualities, we become overwhelmed by the difficulties of life and eventually end up bitter and empty. When we live only in the images of who we "should be," we end our lives in loneliness, without a hint of the power and beauty that lie beyond the surface of life.

We hide from the truth about ourselves because we have made a negative judgment about that truth. We expect others to judge us just as harshly as we do ourselves. So, we become dishonest about who we are and what we feel. The consequence is that we constantly worry about being found out—"If people really know who I am, then no one will like me." Truthfulness with ourselves and others frees us from this terrible fear of others' opinions. When we can face ourselves truthfully, we can easily face others, and we gain self-respect.

Being truthful is the basis for personal integrity. This is a critical element of physical and mental health. When we are inconsistent with what we know to be the truth, we create a subtle weakness inside the body. When we do things we don't believe in or don't want to do, when we say things we don't believe or know aren't true, when our thoughts aren't consistent with our actions, we create an imbalance between mind and body that leads to stress and disease.

This principle also holds true for organizations and the larger society. The less truthful we are as a society, the less capable we are of growing and developing our strengths. We can't solve social problems if we don't understand them, and we won't understand them unless we face the truth of what they are. When leaders mislead, they harm more than themselves, they distort the capacity for effective action; problems are never resolved, and more harm is created. Ego-centered leadership will always put the needs of the individual leader before the needs of those who follow. Truth becomes subservient to the fears and desires of such a leader. But when leadership is based on selfless service, truth becomes the standard rather than the exception.

NONPOSSESSIVENESS: THE ART OF NONATTACHMENT

We saw in chapter 3 that emotional disturbances arise out of attachment to (dependency on) the objects of desire. The greater our emotional attachment, the more dependent we are on a person, thing, action or belief for our personal happiness and the less capable we are of expressing the love of the spiritual Self. Emotional attachments strengthen the grip of the ego-self.

The more I take or own, the more I have to lose. The more I believe I own in my mind, the more my identity gets locked up in material things that sooner or later will disappear from my grasp. Even if I become incredibly wealthy, death will take it all away from me, so what do I really have? It is not having a stereo in my home, or a new car in the garage, that limits me. No thing can limit anyone. It is the idea of ownership that makes me a slave. And we own many things, from material objects (my house, my car, my boat, my roller blades) to people (my wife, my children, my friends) to ideas and beliefs (my prosperity, my religion, my ideas, my God) to actions (my job, my project, my way). The more we own, the greater slave we become to the ego-self.

The ego-self should be a strong, healthy manager, not the owner of the personality. The rightful owner of the personality is the spiritual Self. The way to keep the ego-self from being the owner is to practice nonattachment in all aspects of life. Nonattachment doesn't mean detachment. We don't separate ourselves from life, nor do we deny our emotions and become passive and withdrawn. Nonattachment is the ability to use everything available to us without creating a mental sense of ownership about these things. It is the ability to love someone without having to own that person. Nonattachment means to do the everyday duties we have with focus, clarity and joy, without worrying about the fruits of our actions. Even material possessions are recognized simply as things we may use and enjoy, but not things to grasp or identify with.

The less we burden our minds with possessiveness, the more capable we are of living and working without disturbance. We practice nonattachment when we focus on the here and now rather than worry about what might happen in the future. All too often, when we face difficulties, we become so concerned about what might happen that we diminish our capacity to deal with the problem as it is. Instead, use breath awareness to clear the mind and refocus the attention on what can be done now to solve the problem. By staying in the present moment, we prevent the mind from creating fear or self-hatred.

Another opportunity to practice nonattachment is during arguments. The next time you engage in an argument with your spouse or a close friend, go ahead and argue your point. But while your mind argues, step back and be a witness to your thoughts and behavior. Try to discover just what you think you must have or what must happen in order for you to be happy or satisfied. As soon as you recognize what it is, give it freely to the other person. Don't give it with resentment; that isn't giving at all. Really let go of your attachment to whatever it is you think must happen. Watch what happens to the conversation and the other person's reaction.

There is a great benefit to simplicity. It is the source of the contentment we feel when sitting in an exquisite Japanese garden. There, the simplicity of nature brings clarity to the mind, and we let go of the complications of life. We can turn our minds into Japanese gardens by letting go of the complications that we create through emotional reactions and attachments. The less we own—physically, mentally, emotionally—the more simple life becomes and the greater our inner peace and contentment.

This simplicity characterizes what the samurai call "beginner's mind." When we start a new project or have a new experience, we are caught up in an open-minded fascination. We don't yet know enough to complicate our mind with expectations about what should happen or with attitudes that we have already formed. We simply pay attention and become involved. A "beginner's mind" is uncomplicated, fresh and free from attachments. It is a mind most capable of learning and enjoyment.

To practice beginner's mind, we must pay attention to the moment without being distracted by past experience or future expectations. The more we pay attention to this moment, the less we complicate this moment and the more clear and receptive the mind becomes. When you are doing something, do it 100 percent. The more you wish to be somewhere else, the more you wish something else was happening, the more you anticipate outcomes, the less capable you will be at a given moment. Breath awareness is a wonderful tool for regaining focus. Whenever attention wanders, bring it back by concentrating on breath awareness. When the mind clears, refocus on what is happening now. The true value of nonpossessiveness is a mind that is uncomplicated, free from disturbance and capable of love and compassion.

Through nonattachment, we approach life very directly and very simply. We greet each moment as a new one and each situation with attention and alertness. Winning and losing become irrelevant as self-expression and skill become our focus. If we don't burden our minds with our past hurts, we can approach each situation and each individual with an openness and respect that free us from emotional disturbances. We no longer burden ourselves with a negative history, and life becomes spontaneous joy.

God-centered prayer, meditation and contemplation slowly develop our capacity for nonattachment. As we experience the love, joy and tranquillity arising from our spiritual Self, we no longer need to search for these qualities in the world around us. But we must practice nonpossessiveness and beginner's mind every day. When we do so, our spiritual practices will become more powerful, and realization of the spiritual Self will grow even more quickly. The secret to finding happiness and creating a successful life is to dedicate ourselves to selfless service, to loving others without expectation.

SENSORY CONTROL: FREEDOM FROM SELF-INDULGENCE

All great spiritual traditions emphasize the importance of preventing pleasure and pain from becoming the guideposts of life. Sometimes this emphasis is distorted through ignorance and religious fanaticism. Pleasure is not sinful, nor is pain a punishment from God. Pleasure and pain are information processes rooted in the sensory mechanisms of the body. Pleasure is a signal of sensory (physical) satisfaction or contentment (psychological satisfaction). Pain is a signal that something is out of balance or harmony, either physically or psychologically, and that we should pay attention to discover the source of the imbalance.

When pleasure and pain become ends in themselves, we lose the capacity to discriminate between what is good and healthy for us and what isn't. We begin to seek out physical and psychological pleasure for its own sake. We also expend enormous energy and time finding ways to avoid pain. When this happens, we are completely identified with the ego-self and controlled by the habits of the body and mind.

One of the most powerful sources of both pleasure and pain is sex. Because of this, most cultures attempt to regulate how sexuality is expressed. There are sound reasons for regulating sexual energy and activity. Sexual energy is powerful, creative and joyful. Understood and directed, sexual union can be a resource of physical pleasure, psychological fulfillment and spiritual enlightenment. However, because of the intense pleasure and pain associated with sexual activity, sexuality is all too often the source of dependency, leading to significant physical and mental problems.

Unfortunately, many of the taboos, proscriptions and even laws regulating sexual behavior have little to do with knowledge and mastery and much to do with ignorance and fear. Ignorance of the spiritual foundation of sexuality has led to a distorted emphasis on the pleasure of sexuality, which is the root of our culture's preoccupation with it. Much of what religions have to say about sex only creates greater fear and guilt, leading to even greater distortions. Guilt increases the preoccupation with sex.

Attachment to pleasure and aversion to pain create a materialistic approach to sex. We see this in the distorted prohibitions of religious dogma, in mass media and advertising and in the many absurd laws made by governments to regulate sexuality. Of course, these stimulate reactive forces, such as undisciplined sexuality, promiscuity and the ravings of so-called "New Age" sexual gurus who fantasize about tantric sex and cosmic orgasms. The emphasis on orgasm and pleasure only reinforces our attachments and distorts the ego-self. Pleasure never releases us from loneliness, but only strengthens it.

We must develop a balanced approach, based on a true and thorough knowledge of all dimensions of sexuality—physical, mental and spiritual. Tantric yoga is a highly disciplined path that utilizes all aspects of life to enhance awareness of the spiritual Self. Pleasure is not the goal of tantric sexuality, nor is orgasm. Sensory control is established through specific psycho-physiological exercises and deep concentration and meditation techniques. The sexual organs and glands are understood and brought under conscious control. Spontaneity is achieved through discipline, knowledge and self-discipline and not allowed to be a handmaiden for unregulated urges and sensual pleasure. To lead to spiritual knowledge, sexuality must be based on self-knowledge and self-mastery, not the ravings of an overstimulated imagination.

Sex is not the only problematic area in which undisciplined pleasure and pain lead to emotional disturbances. Many people use food as a source of pleasure, as a way to avoid sexual feelings or as a way to compensate for anxiety. Instead of eating to live, many people live to eat. The consequence is an unhealthy diet, which leads to an unhealthy mind and body. Instead of a proper diet and exercise, people turn to diet fads that promise easy weight loss without discipline. The only real outcome is a monetary gain for the promoters of the diet fad.

The key to sensory control is self-discipline. We cannot impose sexual discipline, food discipline or any kind of discipline. The consequence is repression, fear, guilt and other emotional disturbances, not self-control. Most of us feel that we lack self-discipline. This is not true. We are very disciplined. Unfortunately, we tend to be disciplined in ways that we would consciously choose. Everyday, we worry about the same things, we sit in the same uncomfortable posture, we talk about the same things. We developed these habits unconsciously over time. Real self-discipline is not about making yourself do something you don't like, but rather having the ability to do what you consciously choose to do. In other words, self-discipline is the skill to do what you really want to do. It is the secret to joyful self-expression.

We develop any skill, even the skill of self-discipline, through practice. Self-control comes through self-training. It can never be imposed by priest or preacher, by government or by any other outside source. But sensory control can easily be achieved with the proper training in self-mastery techniques. Prayer, meditation and contemplation are useful tools, but not the only tools. Asceticism (such as fasting), silence, concentration techniques, inspirational readings and experimentation all can contribute to a successful self-training program. All of these tools depend on individual effort, not shortcuts and fads. By taking conscious control over our senses, pleasure and pain become useful tools in our quest for spiritual fulfillment and the end of loneliness.

NONSTEALING: THE PRINCIPLE OF CONTENTMENT

The fifth principle is the principle of nonstealing, refraining from taking that which is not yours to use. When we hear that we shouldn't steal, most of us simply say, "I don't take things that don't belong to me." But like all principles, this one encompasses more of life than what we think it does. Stealing includes taking from others, even by legal means, things we don't actually need. In other words, greed. The principle of nonstealing is violated every day in our materialistic culture.

When we think of greedy people, we think of scoundrels who knowingly grab as much as they can. But greed is often far more subtle, affecting us in ways we aren't even aware of. Advertising agencies hire the most creative people they can to convince us that we must wear the latest fashion, that we won't be happy unless we have the latest in running shoes, that freedom lies in acquiring that expensive European sports car. Every day, politicians and economists tell us to increase our productivity and create more wealth. In other words, we should strive to live the American Dream.

The original American Dream was about freedom of political, religious, economic and personal expression. These brought the original immigrants to the New World. Of course, some, such as the Conquistadors from Spain, came to take as much gold as they could. But the idealistic goal of early America was to build communities in which individuals could practice their own religious and political beliefs without interference from the government. Sadly, this idealism has degenerated into crass materialism and religious fundamentalism. Now the American Dream means to be as rich as one can be, to take as much as one can for oneself and to look out for Number One.

Greed isn't about having things, but rather the need to have things in order to be content, happy or secure. No matter how much we have, greed tells us that it isn't enough, that we should have more. It fuels a desperate race to have more and more. Unfortunately, there is no end to the misery that this creates, for the greedy individual as well as the society. Most of us are so busy making a living that we no longer have a life to live. Many people feel that both parents must work in order to make a decent living. But what we call a decent living is actually quite wealthy—two or more cars, a large home, several televisions, phones in every room. We don't appreciate just how much this high standard of living costs in terms of stress on the family—disease, divorce, latch-key children, the breakdown of communities.

Doing the ten-day exercise mentioned earlier reveals the importance of family, friends, love, compassion and nature. Material things don't even rate an honorable mention. But the treadmill of owning things causes most of us to lose perspective and get caught up in the rat race. But when we take a walk in the forest, in the mountains or on the seashore, we rediscover an inner contentment that has nothing to do with possessions.

On the most profound and subtle level, nonstealing means to be content, to have a refined sense of sufficiency, to know when you have enough. This comes easily when we realize the human spiritual qualities of love, compassion, sharing and communicating.

Why not make contentment an everyday practice? Instead of running to the mall to shop, take your child for a walk in the forest preserve. Instead of buying a new car, why not pay down some debt or invest in your child's education? Instead of reading the latest catalog, why not spend the afternoon helping the local chapter of Habitat for Humanity? The less we depend on things and the more we open our hearts to helping others, the more we free ourselves from greed. Practicing nonstealing is not a chore, it is an opportunity to open the heart—to love, to joy, to contentment.

LIVING LOVE

Being in love is a wonderful feeling, but being Love itself is the most fulfilling experience. When we experience the spiritual Self, we realize a love without boundaries, without conditions, without end. This great Love puts an end to the illusions created by the ego. Loneliness disappears, fear dissipates and self-hatred comes to an end.

We have an unlimited capacity to love because the spiritual Self is unlimited, and we are that spiritual Self. Through Self-realization, we will discover that we are not who we think we are. We are not the sum total of habits and patterns of the mind, the limits and miseries of the ego-self. We are truly children of God, individual sparks of the Divine Light. We should never forget our rightful heritage of love, joy and contentment.

Life is a journey, and the most ancient traveler is love. It is not an easy choice to live with love. To gain our freedom, we must swim against the currents of materialism, and we must wrest control from the powerful ego-self. But we have everything we need. We only need to use our resources to become who we already are.

In the tantric tradition, we greet each other and depart from one another with the phrase "Namaste," with hands pressed together and held over the heart center. This means, "I salute the Divinity within you." Let me say "Namaste" to you. May the spiritual Self be your guide, and may selfless Love light the path before you.